BIRD

WATCHING IN MALLORCA

How, Where & When?
by Neville James Davies

Including tips on motoring,
wildlife and much more...

ecology cymru
ensuring the wellbeing of nature

1st impression

ISBN No. 978-0-9575387-0-2
First published in Great Britain in 2013
© Neville James Davies 2013

Published by Neville Davies (Ecology Cymru - www.ecologycymru.co.uk)
Design & Layout: 1st Impression (Wales) Ltd - www.1stimpressionsigns.co.uk

Cover Design & Titles: 1st Impression (Wales) Ltd.
Front Cover Image: (Hoopoe), ©Alan Woodward
Front Inside Cover Image: (Entrance to Albercutz Farm, from the Formentor road) ©Neville Davies
Back Inside Cover Image: (Section of canal, Albufera Marsh) ©Neville Davies
Photo Credits (Landscapes): Images ©Neville Davies unless stated.
Photo Credits (Birds): Images ©Cliff Woodhead unless stated. Special thanks to Alan Woodward and Cliff Woodhead for their kind contributions.

Original Maps: designed by www.1stimpressionsigns.co.uk
Back Cover photograph: ©Neville Davies

Also by the same author

Birds Of The Caerphilly Basin - Updated version 2009
The Birds & The Bees (The travels of a bird & wildlife enthusiast) - 2012

For copies of the above or to pre-order other publications, please email:
avevigilar@hotmail.co.uk

CONTENTS

ADDITIONAL SITES

TWO ADDITIONAL SITES (if staying on the east coast)

TARGET SPECIES BIRDING

PART FOUR

BIBLIOGRAPHY
PHOTOGRAPHS
ACKNOWLEDGEMENTS
FURTHER READING
USEFUL INFORMATION

ABOUT THE AUTHOR

Born in 1968 in Caerphilly, Neville Davies began taking an interest in natural history in his early teens and became a lecturer of ornithology and palaeontology for adults and school children later on.

He began conducting ecological surveys for companies and private clients about birds, wildlife and plants. The author also organises and leads guided nature walks in the UK, with bird watching tours abroad.

Wildlife talks and presentations are also given to schools and groups (all of which are listed on the website, www.ecologycymru.co.uk).

This is the fourth book the author has written about ornithology, and is the follow up to the 2012 publication, *The Birds & The Bees - The travels of a bird & wildlife enthusiast.*

At present, Neville is busy with ecological work, conducting guided walks and delivering lectures to schools and groups.

DEDICATION

To those brave and gallant people less fortunate than ourselves, who have been deprived the chance to see or hear Mother Nature.

But who will always be in our thoughts and remembered for eternity.

To my partner Nicola
Thank you for entering my life and for being my life

FOREWORD

Visitors to Mallorca are likely to have enjoyed the diversity of birds that the island has to offer for decades. It was not until the 1970s that bird watching was brought into focus by Eddie Watkinson and his wife Pat, with the publication of his booklet entitled 'A Guide to Bird Watching in Mallorca'. In recognition of their valuable contribution to Ornithological knowledge and conservation, one of the hides at the Albufera Marsh bears their name. Through observations, many others have contributed to the store of knowledge about the birds of Mallorca. Along with their enthusiasm they have encouraged others to follow suit. Most notable among these was Graham Hearl who was resident on the island for many years, and whose passion guided the bird watching movement on the island until his death in 2003. It was Graham who organised and conducted the indoor bird meetings in Puerto Pollensa at which residents, holiday makers, visitors and birdwatchers alike were welcome to attend and share bird information.

Graham was assisted by Arthur Stagg also a resident on the island, in the compilation of records, the provision of advice and guiding to visiting birders, and the daily recording of sightings and species from his home base close to the Albufera Marsh. Another close friend of the Hearl household was Mark Thompson. Although not resident, Mark was an equally valuable assistant in every respect to Graham's endeavour. Their passionate approach to bird watching and to the bird life of the Island provided the inspiration to visiting birders and amateur naturalists to submit their observations to a central database. Over the years, the accumulated records numbered many thousands and became the basis for the Ornithological record and history of the island, which stands to the present day.

However, this proud and comprehensive dossier was not restricted to casual recording or occasional contribution. A more scientific approach to bird surveys permitted the accumulation of systematic records, and a fresh and different insight into seasonal and migration patterns, breeding success and population fluctuation. This programme of research was inspired by the dedication and interest of Dave Hanford, ably assisted by David Wellings. Those mentioned here, and many others whose willing help was occasional were no less valuable and appreciated. One of the outcomes of this collective endeavour was an annual report. The Mallorca Bird Reports was initiated in 1990, and produced on an annual basis until 2001. These reports stand to this day as a comprehensive record of bird life on the island for the twelve year period of publication, and have been stored in a secure archive and remain available to any interested party.

For many years, this small group of enthusiasts prepared and set up a small exhibition at the British Bird watching Fair at Rutland Water. Its purpose was twofold. It provided publicity and support for the bird life, wildlife and the environment of Mallorca, often in opposition to development plans and proposals. It also provided support to the work of the NGO, Grup Balear d'Ornithologica I Defensa de la Naturaleasa (GOB). Sadly, the deaths of all of the above named deprived Mallorca, its bird life and visiting birders with services that have been to the benefit of all concerned and in particular to the conservation of birds and their habitats on the island. Reinstatement in the short term seems unlikely.

Ian Tillotson, March 2009

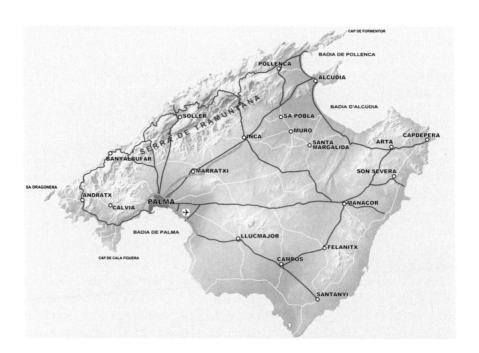

Above: *Island of Mallorca/Majorca - topographic map* ©Intrepix

INTRODUCTION

From an early age I began taking an interest in Ornithology whilst still at school and began going on regular walks with my late father who as a keen Ornithologist from an early age, was in a good position to teach me bird identification skills. Having access to a vehicle meant that birding was not restricted to our local area during my early bird watching days. During my early twenties, the majority of sites visited were within easy proximity of my home and I had accumulated some good records which included Waxwing, Rose-coloured Starling, Mediterranean Gull and Common Crossbill.

I found myself wanting to travel further afield to see a greater variety of species which led me to join a local bird group and take part in organised field trips. I started visiting places further afield such as Norfolk, Scotland, Dorset and Slimbridge. As a result my species list was beginning to grow with 'new ticks or lifers' (terms used by bird watchers to describe a species they haven't seen before). But I wasn't becoming a 'twitcher' however. I was not about to start travelling around the country at the drop of a hat to see a single rare species that had turned up. My preference was to stay in an area for a while and spend more time finding the birds of that location.

As usual each May, my father and I would return to Pembroke for our annual week's birding and walking. It was on one of these breaks in West Wales that we got talking to a bird-watching couple who told us of several trips they had taken to the Balearic island of Mallorca 'but I thought that Mallorca is all beaches and young people getting drunk' I stated. The couple went on to explain about the mountain ranges to be found there, the large marsh areas and the extensive olive groves. More importantly, they told of the many spectacular bird species to be found on the island.

I promised myself that I would visit this island one day to see these wonders for myself. I had pictures in my mind of birds I had always longed to see, especially Hoopoe, Bee-eater and Wryneck. We returned home and as time went on the pull became stronger. I studied Mediterranean species in the books, consulted other people who I knew had been there and eventually visited my local travel agents to find out about prices. I nagged my father to consider a visit there the following May as an alternative to Pembrokeshire as I had a strong urge to see for myself what bird delights the island could offer. In May 1998, we were off - flying from Cardiff to Palma, the island's capital.

I was mesmerised by the beauty of the island and the birds seemed to be everywhere. The light was strong and gave every bird a more colourful and cleaner look. I remember on the first day, about to set off for a day's birding when a Booted Eagle flew over the town, this gave me my first 'tick' of the trip, and what a stunning sight it was too. We saw Hoopoes and Bee Eaters in good numbers - in fact on the first trip we had over a hundred species of which thirty six were 'lifers'. Well for me I fell in love with the island and have returned every year since during the different seasons. Due to driving extensively around the island, finding new locations and re-visiting the main areas countless times, I have got to know some excellent birding sites. I know where a particular rock is used for displaying by a Blue Rock Thrush, or a certain metal post that holds a roosting Wryneck in the evening, arriving around 8.45pm, or which particular shrubs are used for feeding on by Balearic Warblers in the Boquer Valley. I have grown to know the place that well. It is this passion and knowledge which I intend to share with you the reader.

Although I have visited other countries such as Spain, France, Hungary, Poland, United Arab Emirates, Bulgaria and the Greek island of Lesbos, it is Mallorca which draws me back time and time again. This is the fourth book I have written on Ornithology and my aim here is to put together an easy to use and informative guide to allow the reader understand '*How to Bird watch in Mallorca*', and more importantly, where. Through my enthusiasm and passion I hope this is achieved so that you can find all the locations with ease and know in advance how to negotiate the paths when you get there to maximise the number of bird species you potentially see.

Of groves of olives with valleys below.
To mountains above that glisten with snow... Neville Davies

ABOUT THE BOOK

This book has been set out in several parts, with parts one and two consisting of what you can do before visiting the island to familiarise yourself with some do's and don'ts, motoring and local customs. These first two sections therefore will include hiring a vehicle, buying fuel, driving documents, potential driving penalties, the Spanish Police Forces and driving web sites of interest and in part two we look at food and shopping, weather and clothing, language, currency and crime and also a check list of items to take with you.

Part three shows how to use this guide including a systematic check list of the bird species recorded on the island, complete with their Latin names and their status (for example, resident or summer visitor). This section also covers all the main birding sites which I have discovered.

Finally I will offer suggestions for 'target species birding'. If your aim is to simply see the main birds with other species being a bonus or if you only have a set time available, then this section looks at how to maximise your time to travel efficiently round the island to find the specialities which in my opinion would include Spectacled Warbler, Moustached Warbler, Balearic Warbler, Eleonora's Falcon, Black Vulture, Audouin's Gull and Purple Gallinule. Finally there is a complete species 'tick' list for you to mark off the species seen on your trip, to act as both a reminder and a keep sake, and a systematic species list of the birds recorded on the island.

You will notice that I mention Puerto Pollensa numerous times. From a bird watching point of view this is undoubtedly the best location to be based on the island. From here you are in a good position to visit the nearby sites of the Boquer Valley, Postage Stamp Wood, Albercutz Farm, the Harbour and beach, Albufereta and Albufera Marshes. Being based in the north of the island leaves you just one long journey to the Salt Pans which are in the south of the island. Although a little further away Cap de Formentor and Cuber Reservoir are definitely worth a visit, and the driving to both of these locations take you through some stunning scenery with the option of excellent road-side stops for birding.

I have included a section on the Back Roads of Puerto Pollensa as they are of particular interest to the bird watcher and can be incorporated into some pre-breakfast or afternoon birding and also several other local sites of interest.

Target Species Birding (in Part Three) is for those with limited time with information on sites for particular species you may wish to see, which includes some of the islands specialities, and how best to travel around the island to see them.

THE ISLAND AND ITS BIRDS

The Balearics consist of three islands - Ibiza, Menorca and Mallorca. Although Ibiza and Menorca have a good diversity of bird species it is Mallorca which seems to be better known, with around three hundred and forty species of bird recorded. In terms of size Mallorca is 1,405 square miles (3,640 km2). You could fit the island into Sicily seven times over. From its longest point at Sant Elm to the Cap de Formentor is 68 miles (110km). You could fit Menorca into Mallorca five times over. As you approach the island from the air there are several characteristics that catch your eye, such as the extent of the green vegetation below, the strong and clear light and the impressive mountains.

The mountains are important for birds, particularly the birds of prey. There are two ranges one running north to south-west and the other from east to south-east. In the north of the island lies the mighty Serra de Tramuntana mountain range which runs for eighty eight miles from Andratx to Pollenca. Also in the north Embalse de Cuber (Cuber Reservoir) is shadowed by Mallorca's highest mountain Puig Major at 1,477m (4,747ft) home to the magnificent Black Vulture with Puig Massanella following at 1,367m (4,485ft). This same range extends along the left side of the island down to Puerto Pollensa where the Caval Bernat Ridge is equally impressive flanking the left side of the town with the stunning Boquer Valley hidden within it and home to the rare Balearic Warbler.

The island boasts around ten million visitors per year and has a population of around 650,000 inhabitants. The first impressions once on the island are of its sheer beauty its cleanliness and the clear air. As you travel along the fantastic roads you notice the splendour of the homes the large olive groves and open fields and of course, wherever you look the magnificent mountains.

The history of the island

The island has had its fair share of historical action. The first settlers, (around the sixth millennium BC from the south of France) lived in caves and thrived on the abundance of plants and animals. It is believed these settlers were left relatively alone until about 300BC when the Phoenicians began trading here. The wealth and prosperity of the island became common knowledge further afield and perhaps it was only inevitable that the Roman Empire would begin taking an interest in the island's potential. In 123BC they duly invaded and the island began seeing its first Roman roads, markets, temples and villas being established withtThe Romans taking advantage of the islands resources such as olives, grapes and grain.

As a result, the island's economy began to flourish. Gesorix, the leader of the Vandals arrived in Mallorca in the 5th century. The island was annexed by Justinian I, the Byzantine Emperor, in 532. The Arabs finally settled in 902 but the Catalans extinguished all existence of the Moors from 1229 onwards. At this time in the island's history there was both Judaism and Islam beliefs. The island slowly began to settle down under Jaume I, the Conqueror. Finally in 1349, there was a huge battle at Lluc Major, and the island came under the control of Aragon and the Kingdom of Spain.

Today, if one is out birding on the Albufera Marsh or in the Boquer Valley the threat of invasion or capture is thankfully non-existent. The island and its inhabitants have settled down and learned to live together in relative peace and harmony. As a result of its safe surroundings many return again and again. The island offers attractions not just for the bird watcher, but for walkers, photographers, painters, poets and many others with a romantic nature.

The natural history

It is welcoming that the potential for natural history enthusiasts has been recognised and as a result, money has been poured into conservation projects. You only have to look at the new hides and viewing platforms dotted throughout the Albufera Marsh, and the new visitor centre based there, or the Natural Parks of Albufereta and Mondrago which have been established and bear witness to this.

There are also the offshore islands such as Dragonera and Cabrera which are also reserves in their own right. There is a conservation group which has an active interest in the islands birds and the flora and fauna and is known as the GOB (Grup Balear d Ornitologia i Defensa de la Naturalsea).

The best times to visit Mallorca are in April and May when migration is in full swing. The end of April is better however as you have a far greater chance of seeing the arrival of Eleonora's Falcons which are returning from their wintering grounds in Madagascar and also the Bee Eaters and Woodchat Shrikes. Having said that I have visited the island in both the autumn and winter and although the summer species will have gone there are still lots of birds to see as this time of year sees the arrival of a good variety of ducks and waders amongst the many other wintering species.

The Birds

The Balearic Islands as a whole are important for their breeding colonies of Balearic Shearwater and Shag, with good numbers of breeding Cory's Shearwaters, Storm Petrel, Black Vulture, Eleonora's Falcon and Audouin's Gull. Other specialities which can be found on the island at various times of the year include Little Bittern, Night Heron, Squacco Heron, Purple Heron, Little Egret, Greater Flamingo, Red Kite, Marsh Harrier, Booted Eagle, Osprey, Quail, Water Rail, Black-winged Stilt, Stone Curlew, Collard Pratincole, Kentish Plover, Whiskered Tern, Black Tern, White-winged Black Tern, Scops Owl, Bee Eater, Hoopoe, Wryneck, Short-toed Lark, Thekla Lark, Crag Martin, Tawny Pipit, Blue-headed Wagtail, Alpine Accentor, Nightingale, Bluethroat, Black Redstart, Stonechat, Rock Thrush, Blue Rock Thrush, Cettis Warbler, Fan-tailed Warbler, Moustached Warbler, Great Reed Warbler, Melodious Warbler, Dartford Warbler, Sardinian Warbler, Balearic Warbler, Firecrest, Pied Flycatcher, Golden Oriole, Woodchat Shrike, Raven, Serin and Cirl Bunting. Now that is not a bad selection wouldn't you agree?

I hope you have enjoyed the introduction to this book and the island and have an appetite for learning where to see the birds. In the following sections, I have included some points worth remembering about car hire, the local laws and driving on the island.

Above: *Cuber Reservoir looking towards the ridge which is favoured by Red Kite, Black Vulture and Booted Eagle. The stone building with the picnic bench can be seen in the background.* **Below:** *Cuber Reservoir looking towards the Quarry, with the Dam off to the left of the image*

Above: *Looking towards Cap de Formentor. Cases Velles is secluded in between two peaks and is a migration hot spot.* **Below:** *The fields of Cases Velles surrounded by pine forests. This is one of the first areas for migrants to rest and feed and is worth several visits during a stay on the island. The road runs along the edge of the fields so birding here is ideal.*

Above: *The Finca (farm) in the Boquer Valley with the magnificent Cavall Bernat Ridge beyond.* **Below:** *The Boquer Valley showing the thick garrigue vegetation; the best site in this area for Balearic Warblers*

Above: *The Salt Pan workings at Salinas de Levante. The habitat here is a haven for birds with its numerous lagoons and thick vegetation.* **Below:** *Some of the many lagoons at the Salinas de Levante (Salt Pans) which are a haven for water birds and raptors.*

Above: *A small section of the vast Albufera Marsh going off into the distance as seen from S' Illot. This is one of the better winter sites for watching Glossy Ibis and the one and a half million Starlings coming into roost during the winter. During the summer the bird species here can be immense* **Below:** *Albufera Marsh from the Bishop I Hide. This particular area is alive with water birds and raptors*

Above: *The Lighthouse at Cap de Formentor. The cliffs below here are a breeding site for Eleonora's Falcon, Peregrine Falcon and Crag Martin with Shearwaters to be seen out at sea from the balcony* **Below:** *One of the many Puerto Pollensa back roads (looking towards Alcudia). With varied habitats they are ideal for some pre-breakfast and afternoon birding. The phone wire crossing the road is where I watched the Roller.*

PART ONE

VEHICLE HIRE, DRIVING ON THE ISLAND & THE LOCAL POLICE

Where to stay on the island?

Ideally the best place to be based for birding on the island is in the north at Puerto Pollensa. This area is not only stunning but has some great restaurants and amenities and the best place to access the main birding sites relatively easy. As a birding base the best sites on the island are up in the north especially Puerto Pollensa which has the Boquer Valley, Postage Stamp Wood and Albercutz Farm all within walking distance of the town with Albufera and Albufereta Marshes and the back roads all a short drive away. Cases Velles and Cap de Formentor will need to be accessed via a car or bus.

Alternative locations to stay are Cala San Vicente, the old town of Pollenca and Alcudia which is 7km from Puerto Pollensa and the once Roman capitol of the island. Either way vehicle hire is recommended although there is a good bus route system serving all the sites. You will though be restricted to time spent at each location if relying on public transport and having a hire vehicle allows you to stop anywhere along the roadside. This book is based on the fact that you will be hiring a vehicle for the duration of your stay. Once you leave the airport there are two routes to the north of the island. The large road signs appear quickly after you exit the airport so look for the MA-13 road, which will take you straight to Alcudia (and then on to Puerto Pollensa). The second route, the MA-15 road takes you to Arta where you can join the MA-12 road to Alcudia and then join the MA-2200 road for Puerto Pollensa.

There are numerous hotels and apartments in Puerto Pollensa and I have never been unable to find a vacancy. As another alternative you can stay in the east of the island. If based here one would be closer to the Salt Pans and Castle de Santuri but driving would be required for the main sites (the marshes and mountains in particular) both of which are back in the north. There is an excellent bus and coach service on the island. However, personally I prefer to hire a vehicle to get to the sites as I am not restricted to having to rely on bus time tables with the added advantage of stopping any time to see birds that may appear along the way.

When based in the north the only three sites that will require driving to get to are (1) Cuber Reservoir which is a 30km drive along twisting mountain roads from Puerto Pollensa with spectacular scenery and the bird species are well worth it. (2)

Castel de Santuri situated in the middle of the island which is a pleasant drive where in most years an Alpine Swift colony takes up resident around the castle and (3) Salinas de Levante (the Salt Pans) in the south. This site and the nearby Es Trenc are alive with waders and raptor species especially during the spring and summer, and again during autumn and winter, and the whole area can throw up a few surprises as well.

Vehicle Hire

Driving around Mallorca is very pleasant as it has many picturesque places but there are some things though to bear in mind. To really see the islands birding sites in a time scale suitable to the individual, which is usually one week then hiring a vehicle will be necessary to greatly increase your chances of visiting all the sites. Driving does not need to be a daunting experience and providing you take care and don't take any unnecessary risks then driving around the island is very enjoyable. Hire vehicles can be booked in advance of your holiday and collected upon arrival at the airport. Be aware though, if you have booked via a debit or credit card, then this is the one you must provide when collecting the vehicle as the card numbers have to match. It is advisable therefore that you check your cards expiry date prior to booking.

 If you have booked a trip through your local travel agent, then transfer by coach to and from the airport can be arranged in the package deal. Some people prefer to do this on their first visit to the island and hire a vehicle when they arrive at their destination. This will not be a problem as each resort has a selection of vehicle hire firms to choose from. Shop around though for a good deal. When you find the vehicle that suits your needs, it would be in your interest to insure the following checklist is adhered to:

• That the insurance for the vehicle covers your needs

• There must be at least one reflective jacket (chaleco). If stopping on a road for any length of time then this must be put on during the day or night if outside urban areas (these are indicated by street lights and a 50km speed limit). I stopped once on a quiet long open road to quickly take a photograph when a Traffic Officer stopped and I was given a long lecture and narrowly missed a fine. The officer thought I had broken down and I was not wearing my reflective jacket and I didn't have a luminous warning triangle displayed on the road required by law. Next time I made sure I was parked off road on a side track or similar. If the car does not have a jacket, then refuse to leave without one. You are entitled to one. The hire vehicles are fitted with them, and it is better to have one and not need it, than need it and not have it. This does not mean that you have to wear it when birding if parked up off road or in a car park.

• There must be at least one approved breakdown triangle. Some hire companies don't have these in the vehicle and you have to hire them for around thirty Euros. You will be reimbursed with this money upon return of the triangle so this is not a problem.

• If you use glasses for driving make sure you have a pair with you. You may well be asked to show them to a Police Officer if you were ever stopped.

• You must have your driving licence and passport with you when driving. If you don't have these if stopped you may be required to have to leave the car at the roadside to get them and you could be fined.

• There should be a copy of a standard insurance report form in the vehicle (usually in Spanish) and if not ask at the hire desk for one which in the event of an accident must be completed. However, unless you are fluent in Spanish do not sign the form, even if urged to do so by an official unless you are 100% sure that you have completed the form correctly. If you have a camera, take photos from every angle. This will help the rental car company and you with any claims.

Before leaving the vehicle hire office, you should have checked for the following:

• You have insurance to cover the vehicle
• There is at least one reflective jacket
• There is an approved breakdown triangle
• You have your driving licence, insurance and passport with you when driving
• There is a standard insurance report form in the vehicle

Some extra points of note are the wheel trims. You can pay a little more optional insurance to cover damage to the tyres or the trims. It is worth paying the little extra for peace of mind. Some companies remove the trims because of theft. This can however alert the criminal to the fact that you are using a hire car. As in the UK, when you have parked the vehicle, whether it is outside of your hotel or where you are starting a walk from do not leave any items that may be of interest to the opportunist and leave the vehicle in a public area at night under or near street lighting. Although thankfully not common vehicle crime does occur if the opportunity is offered, even in Mallorca.

Take a little time to check engine oil and radiator levels. If the engine is damaged as a result of allowing oil levels to become low then you will be charged. Similarly, check that there is no excessive black or blue smoke emitting from the exhaust. Make sure you keep an eye on the tyre pressure. If you were involved in an accident regardless of whose fault it is and the pressure is low you will be fined. Safe tyre pressures on hire vehicles are 32psi (200kpa / 2 bars). If the vehicle is heavily laden then you will have to compensate for this. Air pumps can be found at all garages and are free to use.

Check with the hire company about the fuel. Most insist that the vehicle is returned with the same amount that was present when you hired the vehicle (usually a full tank) therefore the vehicle must be returned with a full tank.

I tend to get a lot of grit and dust on the vehicle floor by the end of the trip from the many tracks I walk along but don't worry about having to clean the vehicle interior prior to its return as it is included as standard in the vehicle hire price. Finally upon return of the vehicle ask the company personnel to see that you are returning the vehicle in a good condition.

Be aware also of the small print. On a visit in December 2008, and again in May 2009 it stated that the vehicle had to be returned with an empty tank of petrol. When you book the vehicle on-line, you don't actually pay for fuel until you collect the vehicle. The price quoted on-line therefore will be less. When you collect the vehicle you will also be paying for a full tank of fuel. If you can shop around on-line and if possible email the company and query this. I certainly got caught and I don't want this to happen to you. The hire price initially was around eighty Euros for the week but crept up to a hundred and twenty Euros when at the desk which was the added full tank of petrol.

The hire companies are relying on the fact that when you arrive at the airport, you are keen to hire a vehicle and be on your way with minimal fuss therefore many people will simply accept this. This now seems to be standard practice. If you are happy to hire a vehicle with a full tank and therefore have to return it with a full tank, then that is fine.

Buying Fuel

There are petrol stations everywhere on the island especially on the long open roads. Fuel in Mallorca is slightly cheaper than in the UK so if you don't hire a diesel vehicle then you are not going to be out of pocket. If you put the wrong fuel into the hire vehicle however you will be charged for any repairs or damage to the engine.

There are currently around six fuels used in Spain. The most common and the one I always use is the unleaded Sin Plomo (gasinolera). Others include Super 98 octane petrol (for high performance cars), 97octane super (this has a lead replacement which is better for older models), Diesel (gaselino) for all diesel vehicles and Diesel Gaselino A a lower cheap quality fuel. The hire vehicle usually has a sticker either on the dashboard or on the fuel cap area indicating which fuel to put in. It is wise to make sure. Some garages have a person on hand to fill the vehicle up for you but it is more likely that you will perform this duty yourself.

If you are the only person with the vehicle, lock it securely before going to pay the cashier. It is not unknown in Spain (although rare in Mallorca) for an opportunist to take the vehicle if the keys are left inside. Finally, if you have a mobile phone or similar device, do not use it when fuelling up.

Driving licence and documents

Remember when you are driving on the island you must have your driver's licence any insurance documents and your passport with you. Unlike in the UK if you don't have these with you you will not be given the option of being able to produce them within seven days from midnight on the date you were stopped. It is possible that as a result of not having these with you your vehicle will be impounded at the roadside until you can either find a licensed driver or you can produce your documents.

If you are unfortunate to be involved in an accident then it is highly likely that the other driver will be Spanish. Again there should be an accident report form in the vehicle which will probably be in Spanish but do not sign this unless you are 100% sure what the other drivers statement says. Remember to take photographs if you have access to a camera. Include any tyre marks or other relevant marks.

Driving around the island

My first experience of driving abroad was in Mallorca and I remember being apprehensive about it. You have to drive around a roundabout entering it from the right and you drove on the right hand side of the road whilst sat where the passenger would normally be. I laugh now at first trying to change gear with the door handle. It seemed strange driving in a completely different fashion but as time went on it seemed to be easier driving on the right. In fact even now after driving abroad for many years I find it makes more sense and is safer driving on the right hand side of the road. It is surprising how quick you will get into the swing of things and actually enjoy it. Roads are well marked and the journey can be easier if you have someone to navigate for you.

There are two routes on the island however, that do require your concentration at all times and can be a bit nerving when you first drive along them. These are the mountain roads up towards Soller (the route towards Cuber Reservoir) and Cap de Formentor (above Puerto Pollensa). There are regular pull ins along both roads and many hairpin bends. During May especially on the Soller route you will find yourself driving slowly in places as these are the main training routes for cyclists usually training for events such as the Tour de France. They will be in small to large groups but they respect other road users. Their physical fitness and determination is certainly very impressive. Here are some general driving tips:-

1. Road junctions - Remember, you will be giving way to vehicles coming from your left. The only time you will give way to traffic from your right is when there are road side markings, such as on a blind 'T' junction or a roundabout.

2. Roundabouts - You only have the right of way once you have entered a roundabout. Be careful though as a lot of drivers are not aware of this.

3. Heavy traffic - On dual carriageways or the Autopista, if the traffic in your lane has stopped, then you must put your hazard lights on to warn vehicles behind.

4. Flashing red lights - These will usually be on a road side post, and warn of hazards or traffic lights ahead. They can also indicate that you are entering a restricted speed area.

5. Reversing into side roads - Do not perform a turn or a three point turn in city and village streets. 'U' turns can be performed on a wide main single carriageway road if safe to do so.

6. White lines - A single or double white line running along the middle of the road means no overtaking. If you are caught doing this then the fines are heavy and can include penalty points or licence suspensions.

7. Undertaking - On a multi lane highway (Autopista), it is illegal to undertake (pass from the right), unless you are travelling along a signed lane going off to another road.

8. Bus lanes - These are usually found in the large towns with several being in Palma. You can cross one to exit / enter your road, but otherwise only enter them in an emergency, which you have to prove if stopped.

9. Seat belts - These must be worn in the front of vehicles. If seatbelts are provided for the back seats, then these must be worn too.

10. Headlights - These must be used after dusk, dark or in poor visibility. You will also need them when entering tunnels.

11. Overloading - This is a dangerous act. It puts you and other road users in danger and you risk being fined if stopped.

12. Road rage - This is not advisable for obvious reasons.

13. Horns - Do not sound your horn at night especially in residential areas. You will be fined if caught.

Finally, beware of livestock, especially on the mountain roads where goats and sheep can be common. All emergency vehicles have priority. Safely pull over and stop or at least visibly slow down and allow the emergency vehicle to pass.

If you have a normal 'B' licence (over one year) you can hire a moped or scooter if you choose to do so up to a 49cc. If you have held a licence for three years then you can hire a moped or scooter up to a 125cc.

All of this sounds a lot to take in and probably a bit worrying. But relax and enjoy the driving. Remember to take your time and drive carefully. Personally I find driving on the island great fun and relatively easy. I have driven thousands of miles in all weather conditions on the island and because I have adhered to the rules and familiarised myself with the driving customs I have never experienced any problems. In fact I love driving abroad and driving in Mallorca is great fun.

As is the custom in the UK there is no point flashing a vehicle to give it right of way or allow it to pull out of a junction. This is not a recognised act of courtesy in Mallorca or Spain.

If you have however, driven erratically or brought yourself to the attention of the Police in some way then there are penalties if you fall foul of the law such as:

Mobile phones - Only use hands free kits. It is an offence to use a mobile phone whilst driving.

You cannot have any devices in your vehicle other than a hearing aid and this includes blue tooth mobile phones and music players. Fitted car radios are acceptable. **DVD, video or internet screens** must not be used if the vehicle is being used on the highway. Vehicle reversing systems are accepted.

Any child up to the age of three must be strapped into an approved child seat.

The worst road offence in Mallorca is being under the ***influence of drink or drugs***. Spanish Police have seriously clamped down on these offences and penalties are high. The alcohol limits are about half of that in the UK. Simply don't drink and drive. Every officer has a breathalyser device in the vehicle. Any convictions incurred can be passed on to your home authority if you reside within the EU. Spanish Police are also trained to look for the signs of drug use. Failing to comply with a breath test or sobriety test will result in a charge of civil disobedience and often carries a higher penalty, especially if found to be over the limit.

Road signs to look for

CEDA EL PASO	= give way (to traffic from the left)
DESVIO	= diversion
SALIDA	= exit
ATENCION	= caution
PELIGRO	= danger
DESPACIO	= slow
OBRAS	= roadworks

Remember to drive on the right!

There are a few web sites one can look through to gain a better knowledge relating to driving. This information can be found at:
http://www.spainvia.com/motoringinspain.htm

Motoring in Spain (book), by Brian John Deller - ISBN No. 978 84 611 9278 6

This is a third edition book and is well worth a read especially if you are looking to live in Spain or the Balearic islands.

Driving Facts

The speed limit on motorways is 120kph and on main roads 90kph unless signs indicate otherwise. It may seem quite harsh the fact that one can be fined for this or that but all of this makes driving in Spain and the islands much better because the locals also don't want the hassle therefore the driving here is generally very good.

Spanish Police

There are three kinds of Police based on the island, the Policia Local, the Guardia Civil and the Policia Nacional. They are all armed and have their own distinctive uniforms.

Local Municipal Police (Policia Municipal or Policia Local) - The local councils employ these officers, and they tend to work within certain areas for the duration of their service. They deal mainly with minor problems and include traffic issues and control. Their uniform is dark blue with a black and white chequered hat.

Guardia Civil - This is a national force, and specialises in the more rural and country areas, particularly if there are no Policia Local based there. They also perform traffic duties along the highways. They occasionally ride motorcycles and use 4x4 vehicles which are all green and white in colour.

National Police (Policia Nacional) - This force deals mainly with the more serious crime. Their uniforms are brown. They are based in the large towns in a building known as a Comisaria.

PART TWO

SHOPPING, WEATHER, LANGUAGE & CRIME

Food and Shopping

There are plenty of supermarkets with names like Eroski, Supermarcardo, etc. and smaller shops like Spar open daily for food drink and other items. During April to September you will have the pick of restaurants to dine out at. During the winter months this is reduced slightly. Many restaurants are open on Christmas Eve, Christmas day, New Years Eve and New Years day. The coffee shop at Formentor Lighthouse though was unfortunately only open on an occasional basis during the winter although you could still bird watch from here and the drive up is always magnificent.

Weather and Clothing

I have visited the island during December on several occasions and although there is always the chance of rain the temperature has been mild averaging around 8° - 12°. By May however the weather begins to warm up with June to early September being considerably hotter at over 30° C. September and October can be particularly wet months as can April and May. Having said that from the many times I have visited the island the rain has never proved to be much of a problem. I have witnessed some very heavy rain falls and some impressive waterfalls cascading down the ridges as a result. The rain can last for several hours or more but generally rain storms do not last too long. As there is always the chance of rain during your visit it is advisable to pack some waterproofs just in case.

During December although relatively mild pack some jumpers and a fleece. I would advise good footwear during a winter visit as there tends to be surface water around on most footpaths. This is particularly the case at the Salinas de Levante (Salt Pans) and some of the side tracks of the Albufereta and Albufera Marshes. Even during the summer some sturdy footwear is advisable especially on the rough tracks in the Boquer Valley or the walk around Cuber Reservoir.

To lighten your luggage weight if you are taking walking boots, wear them during your flight to and from the island. Daylight hours of course vary throughout the year but from the birding point of view, in late April and especially throughout May, dawn will be around 6.am with dusk at 8.45pm. This works well for me and my clients when out on tours on the island as we can do some pre-breakfast birding from 6.30am to about 8am and have time in the evenings to look for Scops Owls. During the winter months dawn is around 7.35am and sunset around 5.30pm.

The below chart shows a typical temperature outlook annually for the island for the capital Palma, and generally represents to some extent the temperature as a whole for the island and at least gives a general idea of what the temperature range can be.

Majorca has a Mediterranean climate with mild and stormy winters and hot bright summers.

Climate data for Palma de Mallorca													
Month	Jan	Feb	Mar	Apr	May	June	July	Aug	Sept	Oct	Nov	Dec	YEAR
Average High °C (°F)	15.2 (59.4)	15.7 (60.3)	17.1 (62.8)	18.7 (65.7)	22.1 (71.8)	25.9 (78.6)	28.9 (84.0)	29.5 (85.1)	27.1 (80.8)	23.4 (74.1)	19.2 (66.6)	16.5 (61.7)	21.6 (70.9)
Daily Mean °C (°F)	11.7 (53.1)	12.1 (53.8)	13.3 (55.9)	15.0 (59.0)	18.4 (65.1)	22.1 (71.8)	25.1 (77.2)	25.9 (78.6)	23.4 (74.1)	19.7 (67.5)	15.7 (60.3)	13.0 (55.4)	17.9 (64.2)
Average Low °C (°F)	8.3 (46.9)	8.5 (47.3)	9.5 (49.1)	11.3 (52.3)	14.7 (58.5)	18.4 (65.1)	21.3 (70.3)	22.2 (72.0)	19.8 (67.6)	16.1 (61.0)	12.1 (53.8)	9.7 (49.5)	14.3 (57.7)
Precipitation mm (inches)	43 (1.69)	34 (1.34)	26 (1.02)	43 (1.69)	30 (1.18)	11 (0.43)	5 (0.2)	17 (0.67)	39 (1.54)	68 (2.68)	58 (2.28)	45 (1.77)	427 (16.81)
Mean Monthly Sunshine Hours	165	168	204	231	280	307	342	313	228	204	165	154	2,763

Above: *Climate Data for Palma de Mallorca,* Data Source: Agencia Estatal de Meteorología / Wikipedia

Language and Currency

The language of Mallorca is 'Mallorquin', which is a dialect of Catalan. Castellano (Spanish) is also used by all islanders. You will also find that many shop keepers and staff in bars and restaurants can speak a good level of English. If you want to try and speak Spanish when ordering food and drinks or just to speak generally you will find the locals to be accommodating on this and will happily help you if you get a word or two wrong. The Spanish like the fact that someone has taken the time to speak their language. If you fancy having a go then here are some words to learn:

Buenas diaz - good morning, **buenas tardes** - good afternoon, **buenas noches** - good night, **hola** - hello, **adios** - goodbye, **hasta manana** - until later, **por favor** - if you please, **gracias** - thank you, **la cuenta por favor** - the bill please, **uno te con leche** - one cup of tea with milk, **cafe con leche** - coffee with milk, **cafe solo** - coffee without milk, (and probably the most important one) **cervesa por favor** - a beer if you please, **uno** - one, **dos** - two, **tres** - three, **quatro** - four, **cinco** - five, **seis** -six, **seite** -seven, **ocho** - eight, **neuve** - nine, diez - **ten**.

The currency of Spain (and the Balearics) used to be the Peseta but this has now been replaced by the Euro. Prices have steadily increased in Mallorca so shop around for a good car hire rate. There are plenty of car hire firms listed on the internet as elsewhere with big companies being based on the island and at the airport.

Restaurants on a harbour or in the town square will be slightly more than in the town but again look around and compare prices. Hotels will exchange Sterling to Euros for you but the exchange rate will be higher than the banks. There are several different banks on the island including Barclay's near to Café 1919 by the harbour in Puerto Pollensa. When using a cash machine you will have the option of completing the transaction in English. Check however that banks are open during bank holidays or Fiesta days.

Crime

Theft from vehicles does occur on the island albeit uncommon but there are a few simple measures which you can take to hopefully prevent this. Don't leave anything that may be of interest to opportunists. Don't leave any valuables or coats on show. Anything you are not going to take with you when walking or sightseeing place in the boot. I also leave the glove box open to show that nothing of value has been placed inside it. In all the times I have visited the island I have never had a problem with my vehicle by adopting these basic measures. Wherever I am with my telescope and binoculars on show with me, I have never felt intimidated or unsafe. Pick-pocketing and low level theft has been known to occur but usually in the more touristy areas and markets. Ensure that a handbag or rucksack is firmly closed and zipped and not left unattended.

Check list of items to take with you

It is easy to think that you have packed everything you will need only to find that the one thing you need has been left at home. If this is a passport then you won't even be leaving the UK unless you can get it and return to the airport prior to the gates closing. Following is a checklist of items that should be taken with you. The list is not final however and in some examples, items are optional.

Passport (essential for obvious reasons)
Driving licence (including paper section if you have this, although you are rarely asked for this)
Travel insurance (essential) and EHIC medical card
Telescope and **binoculars** (optional)
Camera (with spare film or memory card)
Alarm clock (optional)
Battery adapter / shaver (to run on an 110amp) - Remember to put in a compatible plug adaptor which can be purchased beforehand for use abroad.
Mosquito repellent - This can be bought on the island at any chemist or shop if needed.
Medication - Place in hand luggage if required.
Travel iron (some hotels include these so check their website beforehand).
Clothing (including waterproofs) - Yes it does rain occasionally!
Footwear (general and for walking)
Sunglasses / peaked hat
Bird guide, notebook and pen.
Map, toiletries and **food** can all be obtained on the island.
EHIC medical card - The form can be obtained from any post office in the UK, or simply go online at http://www.nhs-services.org.uk. Most EHIC cards have an expiry date on them, so please check this prior to departure.

Finally, in the unlikely event that you would need it, the **emergency number is 112**. There will be an English speaking operator who can direct you to the emergency service you require.

If you are phoning someone in the UK then dial the following: 00 then the country code 44. Follow this with the area code and then the local number. You usually have to leave out the '0' in the local code. For example Cardiff is 02920 so dialling would be 0044 2920 followed by the local number.

Two bird books I find invaluable and which I always take with me are the Birdwatchers Pocket Guide (Mitchell Beazley), ISBN 0-85533-148-8, price £7.99 which is small enough to carry in your pocket and the more concise Collins Bird Guide, ISBN 978-0-00-711332-3, price £16.99 which is great for more in-depth identification especially with waders, warblers and raptors. There are of course other books available.

PART THREE

HOW TO USE THIS BOOK: BIRD WATCHING SITES & THE BIRDS

Using this book

When you visit a new country abroad even if you have read a map or notes on the location beforehand it can be a lot to take in and finding your way around can be daunting if not a little worrying. Although you may be staying a week or perhaps two it crosses your mind whether you will be to find the sites let alone know where to look for the birds. With this in mind the aim of this book is to show you the reader the quickest routes to where the main sites are and to know exactly where the best spots to find the species within each site are when you get there. A map has been provided for the main site showing the location of key species in the main sites and the routes themselves. All the important sites are covered in this book. I have included some additional sites which are well worth spending some time at particularly if you are staying for more than a week.

For most visitors however a week is usually the only time available to them   Part four offers some more sites again well worth a visit if time allows. Part five looks specifically at target species birding.   Some bird watchers like to look for the star attractions and if all of these are found within their time limits they can then concentrate on finding other species. This section will allow the visitor to achieve this by visiting the main sites set out in the most time and species effective way possible. Part six includes a systematic synopsis of the birds recorded on the island. In part seven we look at the flora of the island followed by a complete species bird list. This has been set out in a more easy to use way starting with the resident species followed by breeding birds, summer visitors, winter visitors, passage migrants, vagrants and finally introduced species or species of uncertain origin. I have included information about the island in part one looking at the history of the island hiring a vehicle, motoring and the different Police forces. I recommend that you take some time to acquaint yourself with this section. Part two will touch on useful information such as food and shopping buying fuel weather and clothing language and currency, crime and a checklist of items you may wish to pack.

Throughout the text you will notice that I have used the roadside 'kilometre markers' as a point of reference in several instances. Signposts are situated alongside every road on the island. They are low white concrete posts with a yellow top. The road number will be on the top (MA) with the kilometre you are currently at underneath. A good road map will complement this book. I recommend the English Edition (updated 2006 after the changes to the road numbers); scale 1,130,000, ISBN 84-8478-081-3.

Finally at the rear of the book I have included my email address to send any bird records to. The directions to all the sites are based on the idea that you are staying at Puerto Pollensa. If however, this is not the case then you will have to refer to a road map. The main sites are listed in order to their proximity travel wise to Puerto Pollensa.

MIGRATION AND THE MAIN BIRD WATCHING SITES IN MALLORCA

Migration

A visit to Mallorca can be worthwhile at any time of the year but if you want to go during the migration period then the best time is between mid April to mid May as migration will be in full swing. This is also the best time for flowers too. Mallorca's main birds are Audouin's Gull, Black Vulture, Balearic Warbler, Thekla Lark, Blue Rock Thrush and Purple Gallinule, which can be seen at any time of the year. Other specialities include Bee Eater, Eleonora's Falcon and Spectacled Warbler - but these are summer visitors. A summary of migrants is as follows:

Spring: Migration is in full swing. In early April it is still possible to see many of the wintering species and the early summer migrants. Birds to look for include hirundines (Red-rumped Swallow, Barn Swallow and Sand Martin), Whinchat, Montagu's Harrier, Black-eared Wheatear and Wood Sandpiper. **April** should also give you other wader species, Spotted Flycatcher, Golden Oriole (Cases Velles), Tawny Pipit (Cuber Reservoir) and Short-toed Lark (Albufera near to the coach park).

The end of **April** will give you Eleonora's Falcons (Albufera Marsh when feeding and Formentor when breeding) and Bee Eater anywhere on the island. **Early May** will give you Squacco Heron (Albufera), Red-footed Falcon and Honey Buzzard especially above the ridges of the Boquer Valley and Cases Velles. By early summer breeding will be well underway.

Return Migration

This tends to start very early with waders passing through from late **July** into early **August**. Water levels are generally lower by this time of year with water birds being concentrated into areas where water collects and sometimes offering great photographic opportunities when close to hides. It is well worth taking the time to scan through the wader flocks as rarities can be mixed in with the commoner species. The Salt Pans, the nearby Es Trenc site and both the Albufera and

Albufereta Marshes are particularly good sites for water birds.

Mid September: Tawny Pipit, Woodchat Shrike and Short-toed Lark will have generally gone. By late October Eleonora's Falcons and Bee Eaters will have also gone. **October to November:** Wader passage is well underway and can consist of a large variety of species. Black Redstarts will also be arriving and will be everywhere on the island in high numbers usually. White Wagtail, Robin and Song Thrush will also be present. Small flocks of Greater Flamingo can occur and Puerto Pollensa Bay is a good spot to look out over the water for this species. They can also be found feeding at the Salt Pans. Sandwich Tern will also be present especially along the harbour walls and exposed rocks at Puerto Pollensa.

Look out for Glossy Ibis whose wintering numbers are steadily increasing. The viewing platform at Salines De Sillot (down from the coach park) is a good spot. I was fortunate to watch six here back in December 2009 feeding close in. Hunting Marsh Harriers will spook the Ibis which take flight and circle around for some time before dropping back into the cover. Stone Curlews can be found particularly on the grass slopes to the right of this viewing platform. Also here at dusk be prepared for an amazing spectacle with 1.5 million Starlings coming in to roost in the reed beds. They swirl and twist in patterns many thousands strong as they circle over the reed beds before descending and their incredibly loud calls are simply spectacular. Definitely worth staying on for after a day's birding.

The six main bird watching sites:

Boquer Valley
Albufereta Marsh
Albufera Marsh
Cuber Reservoir
Cap de Formentor and Cases Velles
The Salt Pans (Sallinas de Levante)

SITE 1:
VALL DE BOQUER -
THE BOQUER VALLEY

Vall de Boquer to give it the correct name is more commonly known simply as the 'Boquer Valley'. To access this magnificent site, head out of Port de Pollensa (on the Formentor Road). Just after where the road changes to one way the Oro Playa Supermarket will be on your left. Turn here and you will see a long avenue of pine trees in front of you. Follow these up along the road looking for Hoopoe along the way. Serin and Firecrest can be found feeding in the pines as can warblers. The pines lead you to a small roundabout. Drive straight over and you will notice an open rough car park to your right. You are now at the base of the Boquer Valley adjacent to what is known as the 'sheep fields'. There is a small brown wooden post marked Boquer.

Spend some time scanning the fields here. A section of the lower sheep fields has been lost to a small relief road but there are still plenty of Almond, Olive and Cork Oak trees to scan through. On one occasion I observed a male Rock Bunting during migration time which was a lovely surprise. You will notice a crumbling stone wall along the left side of the track which has partly collapsed. There is an electricity pole adjacent to it at the start of the wall. During several trips in May around 8.45pm I have watched a Wryneck landing in the 'v' shape at the top of this post to roost on a nightly basis which is very unusual for a woodpecker.

The trees in the field here are ideal for migrants such as Subalpine Warbler, Wood Warbler, Willow Warbler, Bonelli's Warbler, Northern Wheatear, Common Redstart, Pied Flycatcher, Spotted Flycatcher, finches and wagtails including the grey-headed 'iberiae' race of the Yellow Wagtail. In May 1997 I found a male Semi-collard Flycatcher feeding here and in May 1999 I watched twenty three Yellow Wagtails feeding amongst the sheep. This really can be an excellent spot when migration is under way. With patience Wryneck is possible in the Cork Oaks where they blend in beautifully with their cryptic plumage. They also feed on the ground and are the only species of woodpecker to be found on the island.

As you start walking along the rough track, you will quickly come to a rusty gate on the left **(gate 1)** before the first bend in the path. Scan from here as you get a different angle of the fields. In the distance on the far side of the field you will notice a small collapsed building. This is one of the favourite spots for a male

Blue Rock Thrush. Woodpigeon and Turtle Dove feed around the fields. Moving on the path leads around another bend within about fifty feet of the previous one. Scan the bushes and trees around here for Cirl Bunting and Firecrest which are regular. The small tree with a broken limb and dark green foliage down to your right just as you reach the second bend is a favourite calling post for the local Wryneck and two small dead trees on this bend as you look ahead is another favourite spot for Blue Rock Thrushes which chase off the local Blackbirds.

From here the path straightens out and you will see a large metal gate **(gate 2)**. You are allowed to pass through here being sure to close the gate behind you. As this valley leads to the sea it is designated as a public footpath under Spanish law so access is permitted. Just before the impressive Finca (farm) in front of you there are several large green trees on your left (just after the tall Palm trees and Lion statues). Bonelli's Warblers occasionally feed here on passage. The ridge up to your right is good for both Kestrel and Peregrine Falcon with Booted Eagle also possible.

As you continue past the Finca (a request please); it is occupied so please do not stop on the terrace. Quickly move on to the next gate **(gate 3)**. I have seen too many birders standing here for long periods of time scanning out and even eating their lunch on the balcony with some birders entering the front of the house to peer inside. You will get equally good viewing for birds as you proceed through gate 3 and if this practice continues it could cause future problems for birders passing through here. In fact there is already a rumour that the family here are looking to alter the route of the path here.

There are always a few dogs chained up near to gate 3 belonging to the farm. They are secured so ignore them and carry on. There is another gate within fifteen feet of the previous one; this is **(gate 4)**. Pass through this and spend some time scanning the fields below to your left. With patience you should see Stone Curlew which nests in the stony fields below. They blend in very well so may take a little spotting. Red-legged Partridge can be seen also.

The impressive ridge up to your left is the Caval Bernat Ridge and is excellent for raptors which soar above it including Black Kite, Red Kite, Black Vulture, Egyptian Vulture, Booted Eagle, Kestrel and Peregrine Falcon. Pre-breakfast walks to this particular spot to scan this ridge have also produced some great raptor migration early in the morning with Golden Eagle, Bonelli's Eagle and Honey Buzzard all seen on my previous visits. I also watched two Black Storks fly over this ridge in April 1999.   Moving on look for Crag Martins which breed on the cliffs to your right particularly near the section which overlooks the two gates you have just walked through.

As you walk a little further along you will notice the path heads towards two very large and prominent pieces of rock directly in front of you. The footpath runs between these boulders and this is territory to a pair of Blue Rock Thrushes with the male almost always perched on the top of them singing, the cobalt blue of the male looking particularly striking in the strong sunlight. As you walk past these rocks you enter the main part of the Boquer Valley itself which opens out in front of you and for me – always takes my breathe away.

You will be amazed by the beauty of this valley and its sheer size flanked on both sides by high ridges and carpeted by marquis and garigue vegetation consisting of Cistus, Myrtle, Lentisk and Aleppo Pines ideal for feeding and nesting birds. Dwarf Palm (the only native palm in Europe) occurs as does the Hedgehog Plant (Astragalus balearicus).

Sardinian Warbler and Cirl Bunting will be present. It is worth scanning the bushes from here on for Balearic Warbler. **Note:** Balearic Warbler (Sylvia balearica) has recently been split from Marmora's Warbler (Sylvia sarda). The Balearic Warbler is 20% smaller than the nominate form and is paler below with a pink tinge, grey/blue back, red bill with a dark base and red eye (see Helbig 2001, Jonsson and Fjelda 2006).

Further along this path you will notice a small group of pines on your left. Divert off the main track and walk over to these (it is only a short distance). Firecrest, Greenfinch and Serin are regular in here with Red-legged Partridges on the ground below. The latter can be seen throughout the valley as well.

Returning back to the main path keep an eye open for warblers in the abundant thick vegetation and raptor species above the ridges. Eleonora's Falcons can occasionally be seen and Ravens noisily call as they circle above the ridges. There are a small group of Rock Doves which breed here and are regular on the cliff faces to your right. They are of pure wild status.

After walking along for a while the path leads between a dry stone wall with another dry stone wall a little further on **(5)**. As soon as you pass through these walls look for Balearic Warblers. Check every bush particularly on the tops; with patience you will see one or two usually territorial males. This is definitely the best part of the valley for this species and if you wait long enough you will see them.

(6) Further along will bring you to where the path slopes down to the sea. Scan here for Balearic Warbler too as there is always a territorial pair in this particular area but again patience may be needed to see them. If you wish you can walk down to the sea at Cala Boquer where you will see Yellow-legged Gulls and beautiful turquoise waters but I prefer to save time and turn back to return through the valley birding along the way for any species I may have missed. On the return back through the valley take the opportunity to scan above the ridges for raptors which will be using the warm rising thermals above the ridges. Scan above these with your binoculars. Even from the main path an eagle sized bird can at first appear quite small when above these high ridges.

When you return back to the car park, as an additional site you will notice a pine and oak woodland across the road which is Postage Stamp Wood named apparently because of its shape. Golden Oriole can occasionally be found in here feeding during migration but Pied Flycatcher, Spotted Flycatcher, Firecrest and warblers are more regular; Bonelli's Warbler is possible in here. Similarly if you walk away from the car park along the new section of road (to your right as you are facing the town) there is a narrow path leading into a scrub area. This can be good for warblers and Spotted Flycatchers. I watched a group of around three hundred Bee Eaters feeding around here one May afternoon as they were arriving on migration, what a spectacular site!

Winter The numbers of Chiffchaffs and Black Redstarts is amazing. Every bush seems to have movement within it. Apart from Eleonora's Falcons the other mentioned Raptors are still present. Red-legged Partridge numbers seem to increase and can be seen anywhere in the valley itself. Blue Rock Thrush, Cirl Bunting and Hoopoe are still evident but the Crag Martins will have moved to feed over the Albufera and Albufereta Marshes. Sardinian Warblers are still plentiful and the Balearic Warbler can be found in the usual places mentioned. Wintering White Wagtails are fairly numerous. The valley however retains its beauty and magnetism and is well worth a visit during the winter.

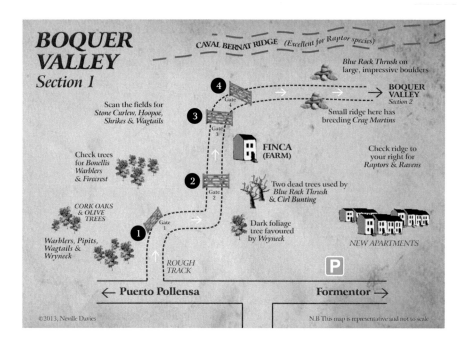

BOQUER VALLEY
Section 1

CAVAL BERNAT RIDGE *(Excellent for Raptor species)*

Blue Rock Thrush on large, impressive boulders

④ Gate 4

BOQUER VALLEY *Section 2*

Scan the fields for *Stone Curlew, Hoopoe, Shrikes & Wagtails*

③ Gate 3

Small ridge here has breeding *Crag Martins*

FINCA (FARM)

Check trees for *Bonellis Warblers & Firecrest*

Check ridge to your right for *Raptors & Ravens*

② Gate 2

Two dead trees used by *Blue Rock Thrush & Cirl Bunting*

CORK OAKS & OLIVE TREES

① Gate 1

Dark foliage tree favoured by *Wryneck*

NEW APARTMENTS

Warblers, Pipits, Wagtails & Wryneck

ROUGH TRACK

P

← **Puerto Pollensa**

Formentor →

©2013, Neville Davies

N.B This map is representative and not to scale

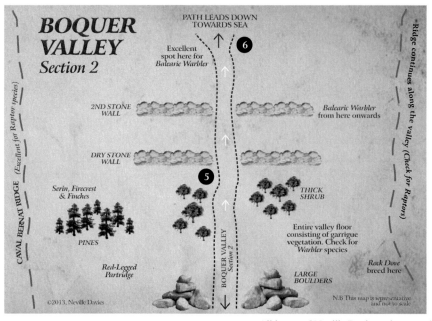

BOQUER VALLEY
Section 2

PATH LEADS DOWN TOWARDS SEA

⑥

Excellent spot here for *Balearic Warbler*

Ridge continues along the valley (Check for Raptors)

CAVAL BERNAT RIDGE *(Excellent for Raptor species)*

2ND STONE WALL

Balearic Warbler from here onwards

DRY STONE WALL

Serin, Firecrest & Finches

⑤

THICK SHRUB

BOQUER VALLEY Section 2

PINES

Red-Legged Partridge

Entire valley floor consisting of garrigue vegetation. Check for *Warbler* species

Rock Dove breed here

LARGE BOULDERS

©2013, Neville Davies

N.B This map is representative and not to scale

All images ©Neville Davies unless stated

SITE 2:
S' ALBUFERETA ES GRAO -
THE ALBUFERETA MARSH

This has recently been adopted as a 'Parc Naturel' (Natural Park) which is great news conservation wise as it is a magnificent area for birds. Leave Puerto Pollensa and head towards Alcudia on the MA-2202 road which runs alongside the sea. As you are driving towards the Km65 post keep looking to your left as the beach regularly holds small numbers of Audouin's Gulls amongst the Yellow-legged Gulls. Shag can be seen out on the rocks. Just after Km65 you will drive over a bridge where the cycle lane and hard shoulder on the right becomes noticeably wider for a short length. Immediately on your right are a row of houses. Turn into here onto the road which in effect doubles back on you. Now you will be facing Puerto Pollensa. The turning is a bit tight so if you miss it drive on for a short distance where the road becomes wider and drive back.

Once you have parked by the houses in the open space before proceeding along the main track to your left walk directly ahead into the vegetation adjacent to the road barrier above you. There are a set of concrete steps here from which one can scan the water and mud in front of you.

The bridge you have just driven over has water flowing underneath it which is tidal fed from the sea and brings in an abundance of food for a variety of water birds which can be found here. It is well worth a look for Little Egret, Purple Heron and waders. I have seen Common Redshank, Ringed Plover, Little Ringed Plover, Kentish Plover, Purple Heron and Turnstone (the latter being rare on the island) at this spot. On one special occasion I watched a male Ferruginous Duck on the water here my first ever sighting of this species. There is always a good selection of waders feeding here.

Go back to your vehicle and start walking along the main path **(1)**. The small area of scrub to your left always holds Sardinian Warbler and the pine trees on your right have Serin, Greenfinch, Chaffinch, Firecrest and House Sparrow in them. Also check the first field to your right for Kentish Plover which breed in this area. Views of this species can be excellent in this field, ideal for photographs. Stonechat is always present and these fields which are usually tilled can also attract wagtail species.

There is a newly built house with a blue front to your left. Check the scrub just past this as a small colony of Tree Sparrow can be seen here mixing in with the local House Sparrows. A little further along this path there is a ditch running both sides of the path **(2)**. The ditch always contains water which has a steady flow being a section of the Torrente de Xante. Green Sandpiper can sometimes be seen here as can Water Rail.

Walk past the pines on your left which are good for Common Whitethroat and Woodchat Shrike. There is a nice 'limestone pavement' here filled with Asphodels and several species of Orchid so please be careful if you walk around here. Continue on with the dry stone wall on your right for a short distance until you can see another wall branching away to the left. Corn Bunting and Fan-tailed Warbler can be seen around here and expect to start seeing Marsh Harriers hunting over the fields and open water.

Continue walking to your left so that the pine trees are on your left and you will shortly come to two dry stone walls **(3)** with a narrow path running between them. Begin scanning the open water from here on the right (before walking between the walls) for Purple Heron, Grey Heron, Little Egret, Cattle Egret, Great-white Egret (in winter though occasionally in the summer months too), Pochard, Mallard, Teal, Shoveler, Pintail, Tufted Duck, Coot and occasionally terns such as Whiskered Tern, Common Tern and White-winged Black Tern. Marsh Harrier, Kestrel, Eleonora's Falcon and Osprey can all be seen from here.

Follow the path between the two walls to the end (a short distance). Sometimes there is a wooden gate across the path only to prevent the sheep from escaping but you are allowed to walk through closing it behind you. Now you will notice open water both to your right and left and a good scrub area in front of you. The scrub can be good for Thekla Lark, Hoopoe, Stonechat and Woodchat Shrike, with a variety of warblers feeding here too. Scan the water to your left first for ducks waders and Black-winged Stilts. Corn Bunting favour the Tamarisk bushes alongside the water's edge and a few males can always be heard calling, with the distinctive 'jangling keys' sound.

Walk a little further on to a spot known as 'the raised mound **(4)** but it is not an obvious looking mound so use the mountain peak and the masts in the background to show you are in the right spot. This is a better spot to scan the larger expanse of open water in front and behind you. Herons, waders, terns, ducks, egrets and the occasional Collard Pratincole can all be seen from here. This is an excellent spot to scan for Eleonora's Falcons which feed on the abundance of Dragonflies over the marshes. Osprey are usually present here especially perched up on the short posts dotted along the waters edge. Great-white Egrets favour this area too with one or two present in the summer and numbers rising during the winter months.

A short distance away there is a small stone building with a large Prickly Pear growing in front of it. Sardinian Warbler and Chiffchaff favour this tree. Corn Buntings are always close by and in the fields to the left of the building nesting Stone Curlew can sometimes be seen. These fields also hold Quail amongst the lines of crops. They are incredibly hard to spot but can sometimes be heard. Please do not be tempted to enter these fields. They are private and there will be a risk to the nesting Stone Curlew and Quail.

You have to return along the same route back to the car but this allows you to scan the water and fields from a different direction and perhaps see some more species.

Winter birding: Marsh Harrier, Osprey and Kestrel are always hunting here. Hoopoe, Thekla Lark and Kentish Plover are still present. The water areas hold large numbers of wintering duck including Mallard, Shoveler, Teal, Wigeon, Coot, Pintail and Red-crested Pochard. There are usually at least three Great-white Egrets present with occasional Squacco Heron plenty of Grey Herons and a few Cattle Egrets mixed in. Little Grebe, Kingfisher and Greylag Geese can all be found. In just over an hour here in December 2008 I saw over forty species so there are still plenty of birds about. Fan-tailed Warbler, Reed Bunting and Linnet will be present.

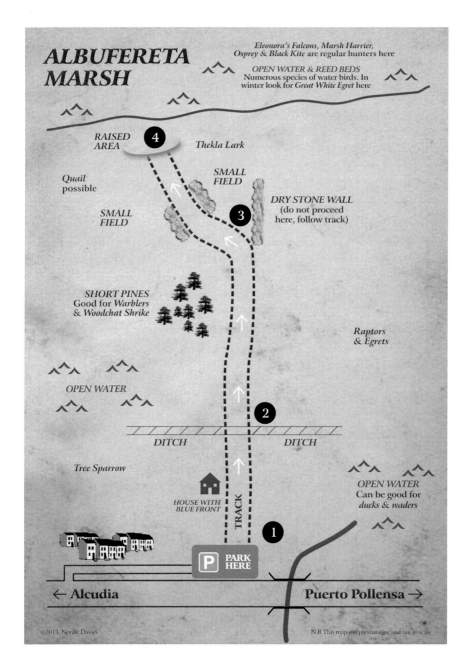

All images ©Neville Davies unless stated

SITE 3:
PARC NATUREL DE S ALBUFERA DE MALLORCA - THE ALBUFERA MARSH

Pliny once wrote of 'Night Herons, being sent to Rome as a gastronomic delicacy' from this area. To bird watchers however this site is simply known as The Albufera Marsh. It is the largest and most important wetlands area in the Balearics and also has the most important ecosystem. Once a former lake it became separated from the sea by a line of sand dunes becoming a large swamp which was drained in the 1860s. It is possible to spend a whole day here and expect to see in excess of sixty or so species of bird during a summer visit (late April and early May especially). The Albufera is a vast area which becomes evident when you look out from the viewing platform at point 4. If you desire you can visit all the hides on the marsh but some paths are very long and species seen from these hides can easily be seen on the easier and more time friendly route which I have set out and personally follow when I visit. This will allow you time to visit a nearby site (S Illot) which looks over a different part of the marsh and has two viewing platforms and are definitely worth a visit.

The Albufera was declared a Natural Park on 28th January 1988. It has a surface area of 1,646 hectares. Parts of the grassland here developed during the Tertiary era with the wetlands forming around 100,000 years ago. The coastal dune system however formed around 10,000 years ago. Common Reed and Fen Sedge form the bulk of the vegetation here along with Reedmace and Glassworts. Over 10,000 birds spend the winter months in the Park and three hundred and three species have been recorded here so far.

The Park is open from 9am–6pm from April 1st to 30th September and from 9am–5pm between October 1st and 31st March. However the gate at the main entrance has a short wall which acts as a style and access to the Park therefore can be on any day of the year. I have been here on Boxing Day and the hides can still be accessed too. Entrance to the Albufera is free but once you reach the visitor centre please make yourself known and pick up a map and permit. This helps with the footfall of visitors to the park and helps towards funding. Also one can obtain leaflets about the area and toilets and cold drinks are available (hot drinks via a machine). Entrance is permitted only on foot or by pedal cycle.

If you are having to rely on buses during your stay then from Puerto Pollensa adjacent to the harbour one can catch the number 2 bus which goes past the entrance of the reserve. There is a bus every twenty minutes and the cost is 1 Euro 75 for a single ticket. Ask the driver to stop at the entrance of the reserve. The return bus stop is on the opposite side of the road by the entrance of the reserve.

To get to the Albufera by car, head out of Puerto Pollensa on the MA-2202 road, towards Alcudia. You will pass the route you took to the Albufereta Marsh along the coast road. Continue on to the roundabout. Take a left here and head up to the top of the road. Follow the road around to the right (the castle will be on your left) and stay in the right hand lane to the traffic lights just ahead. Turn right at the lights and head down past the Roman remains and ampetheatre. At the roundabout take a right sing- posted Arta and travel past Burger King and numerous shops. This 7km stretch of straight road (speed limit 50km) is Alcudia itself. There are several roundabouts on this road but go straight ahead to the very end.

As you leave the main built up area you will drive over a bridge with a large canal below. Immediately after this bridge (known to birders as the English Bridge) take a right and park in the small car park provided (free parking) by a set of traffic lights. If this is full parking is permitted along the residential roads adjacent to the Albufera but check any signs if they are present.

Dawn at the marsh is a wonderful experience and the 'dawn chorus' of countless species is breathtaking. If you are entering the reserve with a pushbike you will not be allowed to cycle further than the reception area although walking is of course permitted and you can push the bike around.

Once you have parked your vehicle in the small car park off the main road follow the narrow sandy path through the pine trees back towards the bridge you drove over. Cetti's Warblers will immediately become evident with their loud calls. Turn in on the main track left into the reserve and proceed through the gate (1). Check the large pines immediately to your left. A colony of Little Egrets nest in these tall trees. Serin, Spotted Flycatcher, Chiffchaff and Willow Warbler can all be found. Continue along the straight tarmac path checking both to the left and right for Marsh Harriers, Cettis Warbler and Egrets. The canal on your right is Canal Siurana with several wooden platforms which project past the scrub and allows you to scan up and down the canal. Red-crested Pochard, Coot and Moorhen are all evident and the line of Tamarisk and other bushes along the waters edge on the opposite bank hold Night Herons which roost in the open by day and offer excellent views. Check the pylons for perching Osprey.

Where the track bends to the left (**2**) there is a small bridge. Check the water here on both sides as this is a good spot for seeing Little Bittern. Moustached Warbler (of which there are around 3,000 pairs on the reserve) can also be seen. Before continuing on the path (which immediately bends back to your right), scan the marshy pools. Marbled Duck seem to prefer this area and a pair actually bred here in 1997. Purple Heron and waders can all be seen and keep an eye out above for raptors especially Booted Eagle, Eleonora's Falcon and Osprey. You will notice hundreds of hirundines aerial feeding. They mostly consist of Swallows, House Martins and Common Swifts but scan through them for Red-rumped Swallow, Pallid Swift and occasionally Alpine Swifts which mix in with these flocks on migration.

On your right is a raised boardwalk which offers good views onto the open water. There are numerous open areas of water amongst the rushes and reeds so scan through any duck and wader species for rarer ones which stop off to feed during migration.

Just after the boardwalk is the reserve centre (times vary on opening, 9am-7pm in the summer and 9am -5pm in the winter). Remember even if the centre is closed access is still permitted around the reserve. There are display boards here toilets and a drinks machine. Have a look in the pines opposite around the picnic benches. Firecrest, Nightingale and Serin use these regularly and I have also had Bonelli's Warbler feeding in here.

(**3**) Just on from the reserve centre take the narrow path leading off to the left under some large trees and head towards the CIM hide. Check the open field to the left for Iberiae Wagtail, Yellow Wagtail, Stone Curlew and occasional Collard Pratincole. From the hide there are plenty of birds to be seen on the lagoon particularly Purple Gallinule which were re-introduced here from the Coto Donana in 1991 in an effort to re-establish the population due to them being previously hunted to extinction in Mallorca. They now thankfully enjoy safety within the Park and numbers are steadily increasing. Their progress has been well received and Gallinules are regular at other sites such as the S Illot and Tucan Marsh - a real success story.

Several pairs of Marsh Harrier are always evident from here as are Black-winged Stilt, Purple Heron, Little Egret and wader species. Tern species such as

Whiskered Tern, Common Tern, Black Tern and White-winged Black Tern can sometimes be seen from this hide. There is always plenty of bird life on this lagoon offering close views.

When you leave the hide head back towards the main track but follow the narrow dirt track this time around to your left and underneath a group of large mature Plane trees. Walk past a series of solar panels on the ground to your right and up over a small wooden bridge. Check for Moustached Warbler here and possible crake species.

In front of you are a set of wooden steps leading up to a raised circular viewing platform **(4)**. Here you will truly appreciate the sheer size of the marsh. Marsh Harriers will be evident in good numbers hunting over the expanse of reed beds but keep an eye out also for Eleonora's Falcons sometimes in large groups aerial feeding on Dragonflies. They twist and turn sharply in pursuit of their prey and are very impressive to watch. Look for Great Reed Warbler, Moustached Warbler, Nightingales and Little Bitterns, the latter criss-crossing over the narrow canals.

Walk back down the steps and head towards the holding pens with a small adjacent pool and information board. This is where any re-introduced species are housed. This has included White-headed Duck and Crested (red knobbed) Coot. The Crested Coot is still present on this pond and allows close photographs. There are a few pairs however which have left this area and can be found on the canals around point 5. I am not sure if these are now classed as wild but they are free flying birds and are breeding. Definitely of wild status though is a male Great Reed Warbler its song being far carrying and distinctive and this particular set of reeds and small pond forms its territory. The song is very loud and can even drown out the local Nightingales. With patience you will see it as it sings from the top of the reed stems which bend over as it does so. Reed Warbler and Sedge Warbler can also be seen around here. A small information board shows some of the re-introduced species.

Continue on towards a path which leads onto one of three small stone bridges **(5)**. From the first bridge start to keep an eye open for snakes which frequent the water below. The second and largest bridge is a good viewing place for Cettis Warbler, Moustached Warbler, Reed Warbler and Great Reed Warblers. A track just before here to the left takes you to the Watkinson Hide. It is a relatively short walk to this hide. Little Bittern can be seen here especially in the early mornings but apart from duck species which you will have already seen; there is not much else to be seen from this particular hide.

In between the second and third bridges a path again leading to the left will take you to the Tower Hide. This was once a high wooden viewing platform which shook unnervingly as you climbed the steps but has since been replaced with a more sturdy metal and wooden structure. It is quite a long walk to this hide but views over the park are good and in 2002 I watched a Trumpeter Finch feeding in the vegetation below and Eleonora's Falcons can be watched catching Dragonflies in the direction of the power station.

Staying back with the bridges (just before the third bridge) check the small open area of water slightly right of the end of the bridge. This is an excellent spot for Moustached Warbler and usually the only place on the reserve I can guarantee to see them providing one is patient. It is certainly a nice spot to have a break for a while and perhaps some lunch. Snakes can be seen from here in the canals below.

A narrow path runs through an avenue of dark coloured trees and bushes. There are two hides along here well worth a visit - the Bishop I and Bishop II Hides. Nightingales and Cettis Warblers are abundant along this path offering a good chance of actually seeing them relatively close with the sighting being of the usual flash of chocolate brown as they flit across one side of the path to the other. You will certainly hear their distinctive calls if nothing else. With patience though both species will feed or sing in the open and then their delicate plumage and far carrying songs can be appreciated.

You reach the Bishop I Hide **(6)** after about 350m. Spend some time in here. In front of the hide will be breeding Black-winged Stilts. Bluethroat are possible here and elsewhere in early spring as are Black-tailed Godwit. The habitat in front of this hide is one of the best sites for Marsh Sandpiper in spring. During May keep a look out from here for Collard Pratincole, Little Ringed Plover, Ringed Plover, Kentish Plover, Curlew Sandpiper, Ruff, Greenshank, Wood Sandpiper and other wader species. There are several short posts in the water further out which are regularly used by perching tern species. Hoopoes are always present flying back and forth in front of the hide.

A number of bare low bushes beyond these posts can hold Kingfisher, Bee Eater and even a resting Osprey. Marsh Harriers will be flying around here and in the direction of the power station look for Eleonora's Falcons feeding usually in good numbers. Again check through any hirundines present for Red-rumped Swallows mixed in. During one early morning visit I watched a Little Crake walking to the left of the hide in the shallow mud.

When you return to the path an option is to turn left and walk for about 150m to the Bishop II Hide. This offers a slightly different angle over the marsh **(6a)**. If the Osprey is around it can be seen closer in from this point. There is also the chance to check over more water areas. From both hides the abundance of water birds are staggering.

When you return back to the bridges you have the option of walking down the long path to the right to the Es Colambars Hide **(7)**. Little and Cattle Egrets can be found here along with occasional wader species and Marbled Duck. Either way when you return to the bridges take the short path to the left which runs alongside the small canal towards a wooden bridge. Walk over this and it brings you back to the visitor centre. Return the same way to the car park birding as you go of course.

Winter birding: It is definitely worth a visit to the Albufera during the winter as species of ducks and waders increase. Night Herons can still be seen roosting in the bushes on the opposite side of the large canal as you walk in to the reserve. Cetti's Warblers are easier to see as there is less cover. Cormorants (which winter here) are numerous. Any patch of reeds will have several pairs of Marsh Harriers hunting over them. Chiffchaff and Robin will be evident. From the CIM hide (point 3) there are large numbers of Shoveler present (over 500 in some winters in front of the hide) along with Pintail, Teal, Mallard, Red-crested Pochard and Gadwall.

Common Snipe, Jack Snipe, Black-winged Stilt and Common Sandpiper are likely with Green Sandpiper also a possibility. Purple Gallinule, Grey Heron (winter visitors) and gulls will be present including Yellow-legged, Black-headed and occasionally Audouin's Gulls. From the Bishop I Hide, look for Osprey, Kingfisher, and waders (I have seen Spotted Redshank from here). Little Egrets will be present in good numbers. The mud usually to the left of this hide can be good for Water Pipits and keep an eye out over the open area in front for wintering Hen Harrier which occasionally hunts here. Black-necked Grebe and Spoonbill are also possible in winter.

Depuradora De S' Illot (waterworks)

It is well worth visiting this site throughout the breeding season as an addition to the Albufera. The Depuradora (or waterworks) is an area packed with birds. To access it once you have returned to your vehicle at the small car park by the entrance of the Albufera take a right onto the main road and continue along through the avenue of pines (and away from the town of Alcudia). Keep an eye out on your right first for a track which goes in by a small waterworks building with an area of water in front of it (about a quarter of a mile past the car park you have just left). This is not the main waterworks site of S Illot but is well worth a stop off en-route. Spotted Crake has been recorded here and it is worth spending a little time here to see what may have turned up on migration. The telephone wires regularly have Woodchat Shrike and Bee Eater perching on them.

Continue on the main road until you eventually come to a roundabout. Take the first exit right sing-posted Muro and Sta Magalida. At the next roundabout (immediately after) take another first exit right sing-posted Muro and Sa Pobla. The road will bend around slightly left and then straighten up again.

On this straight stretch look for a right turn (approximately 300yds) where there is a large building with nine metal shutters on the front **(1)**. This is the coach park/workshops. Follow this tarmac road along but drive slowly as there are lots of birds to be seen and large open fields to scan for harriers. You will begin to notice Woodchat Shrike and Kestrel immediately - usually perched up on the telephone wires. Bee Eaters breed in this area and can always be found perching on the telephone wires or flying around in search of Bees, their favourite food. Turtle Dove can occasionally be found here. Check over the open fields for Hoopoe.

As you continue along you will soon drive alongside an area of boulders on your right **(2)**. Stop here for a while and scan amongst the boulders. This is a good spot for Short-toed Lark and Northern Wheatear the latter being in good numbers during migration.

Driving on past several small houses on your left you will come to a chain link fence also on the left with a dark green hedge running alongside it. This is the perimeter fence of the waterworks site. Turn in here and drive along the dirt track. Follow it along to the end where there is a viewing platform **(3)** which has replaced the original low wooden hide. Once up on the viewing platform you will see Marsh Harrier and Eleonora's Falcons which will be hunting and feeding over the marsh but check on and around the edges of the five lagoons in front for birds such as Stone Curlew, Marbled Duck, Black-winged Stilt, Whiskered Tern, Black Tern and White-winged Black Tern. During 2008 I watched two Gull-billed Terns flying around these lagoons. Squacco Heron, Collard Pratincole and Garganeye can also be seen. Hirundine numbers will be high so again check through them for smaller numbers of Red-rumped Swallows. Pallid and Alpine Swifts may also be present. There is usually Common Sandpipier and Common Redshank present along the edges.

There have over the years been some interesting records from here consisting of 'vagrant' species such as Oystercatcher, Caspian Tern and Red-Knecked Phalarope. Being a part of the fenced off waterworks site birds are left in peace so the chances of some special birds are good. This is one spot on the island where some of the rarer waders such as Turnstone, Knot and Sanderling can sometimes be seen. Stonechat and Nightingale show well from here amongst the thick vegetation below the viewing platform. Kestrel regularly hunt over the fields on a regular basis.

Returning to the tarmac road you turned in off take a left and drive just past the entrance of the waterworks and park on the sharp corner where the road bends around to the left **(4)**. I have seen Black Kite in this area on several occasions during April and May. Great Reed Warbler and Cetti's Warbler are regular around here and Purple Gallinule is always present usually running into cover upon ones arrival. Follow the path towards the house. The area off the path can be quite damp and regularly has several Common Snipe which fly up at the last minute as one walks past. There are usually two chained up dogs here and please out of respect walk past the house as quickly as possible. It is occupied and the family like to eat their food outside which is customary on the island. However during 2011 the place was deserted but by now I am sure it will have been re-occupied.

Move on to a wooden gate with a climbing stile either side of it **(5)**. The small field and vegetable garden just before it can be good for finches and wagtails. Before climbing over the stile check the water way to your right and left for Moorhen, Purple Gallinule, Little Bittern and Water Rail. Once over the stile scan over the open water slightly away to your left. Marbled Duck and White-headed Duck can be seen here. In May 1998 I watched a Ring-necked Parakeet flying around here. As you walk towards the derelict farm house on the right check the open fields around it for Blue-headed Wagtail, Cattle Egret and Squacco Heron. The house holds many pairs of nesting feral pigeons which are increasing every year and probably explains the more regular occurrences of Peregrine Falcon in this area. After heavy rain a temporary pool forms next to the house which can have wagtail and wader species present.

Head towards another gate a little further along this path (6) with large pine trees adjacent to it. To the left of this just before the gate is a viewing platform with good views over large expanses of the marsh. The introduction of a small herd of horses from the Carmargue region of France helps to keep the water area open and of course muddy ideal for a variety of waders and ducks. Purple Gallinule, Purple Heron and Little Egret favour this area. Harrier species are always present and both Cettis Warbler and Sardinian Warbler will be feeding around the vegetation by the platform.

It is worth spending some time on this platform. The grass area to the right apart from having Rabbits feeding on it, is also good for Stone Curlew, Hoopoe, wagtails and pipits. The fence beyond regularly has perching Whinchat and Stonechat on the posts and wires with the occasional Northern Wheatear. The long path leading away to your right takes you into the Albufera Reserve. However you will have covered that area during a visit to the reserve itself.

Before returning to your vehicle, have a look around the large pine trees adjacent to this platform. Firecrest, Serin, Willow Warbler, Chiffchaff, Common Redstart, Woodchat Shrike and Spotted Flycatcher are regular feeders here and to the right of these trees are small pockets of water where duck species can be seen. Hoopoe are regular here especially around the derelict buildings.

Winter birding: Beginning again on the track from the main road (1), drive slowly and keep an eye out for Hoopoe, Kestrel and Stonechat. (2) Thekla Larks can occasionally be seen here along with good numbers of Linnet, Greenfinch and Goldfinch. (3) As you drive along the dirt track towards the first viewing platform scan the fields to the left for large numbers of Skylark which winter here. Corn Bunting should also be present. Shoveler and Mallard are usually present on the lagoons with both Common Sandpiper and Green Sandpiper a possibility. (4) After a lot of rain there are always small pools before you reach the inhabited house where Common Snipe and occasionally Jack Snipe can be seen. Purple Gallinules will be running into cover. Look out for Water Rail both here and when you approach point (5). There is usually water present around the derelict farm house as well where waders can be found especially Lapwings.

Spend time on the viewing platform as there are a number of species out on the marsh such as Purple Gallinule, Teal, Shoveler, Wigeon, Pintail, Shelduck, White Wagtail, Water Pipit, Black-winged Stilt and both Common and Green Sandpipiers. Kingfisher and Hoopoe will be around as will at least four pairs of Marsh Harriers. Keep an eye out for Hen Harrier as well.

I suggest spending time here during a winter visit as Glossy Ibis will be seen with patience. The area holds around half a dozen or so wintering birds and sooner or later they fly up having usually been scared by the hunting Marsh Harriers or Booted Eagles. The Ibis will circle for several minutes before finally settling down again and out of sight in the thick reeds. During December 2008 I counted nine here. Also from this platform around 4.30pm onwards you can watch a truly epic spectacle of over a million and a half Common Starlings coming into roost in the reed beds. When you put your scope or binoculars onto each dark shape in the sky you will notice to your amazement that there are so many more birds than you first imagined. They perform magical shapes as they twist and turn before descending into the thick reeds to roost. As they gather so do Sparrowhawks and Peregrines Falcons albeit in ones or twos hoping for a last feed. The Starlings make an incredible noise when they are settling down, and occasionally take flight for a while again as a Marsh Harrier comes too close. The noise continues for quite some time, and then suddenly, all goes quiet. But what an amazing spectacle to watch!

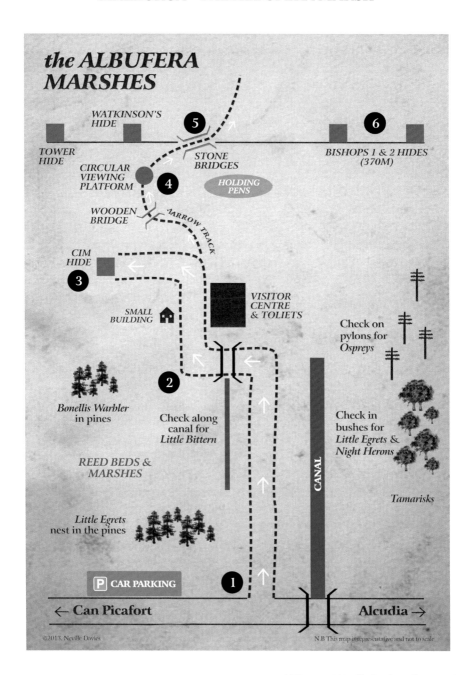

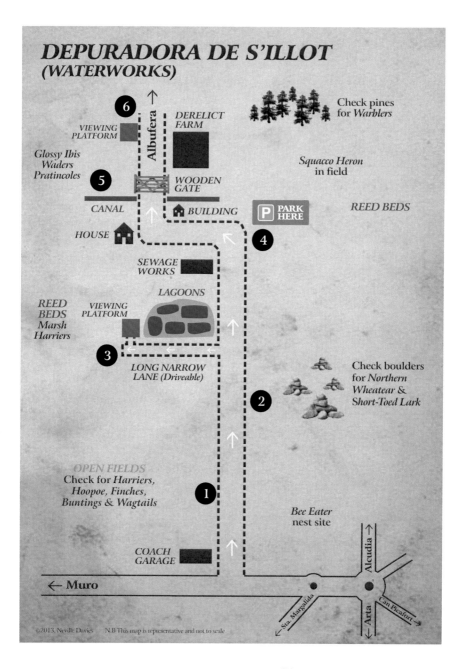

SITE 4: EMBALSE DE CUBER - CUBER RESERVOIR

To reach Cuber Reservoir travel out of Puerto Pollensa on the MA-10 road. Continue straight past the turning for Cala San Vicente and up to the main roundabout. Beyond the roundabout the road straightens out for some time before climbing steadily uphill. The ridges to the left of this road are favoured by light and dark phase Booted Eagles. The drive up to the reservoir at Cuber is about 30km. The scenery is spectacular. The roads twist and turn around a series of hairpin bends and the bird life is amazing. Take care as you drive along this route for goats and sheep which can appear suddenly on sharp bends.

During April and May you will see groups of cyclists slowly making their way along this road many of whom train here for the Tour de France and other major events. They pass Cuber and continue on down to Soller. Be sure to check your rear view mirror before slowing down to look at birds to prevent other motorists or cyclists going into the back of you. I would suggest avoiding Cuber Reservoir itself on a Sunday and Christmas Day as it can be quite popular with locals and although species can still be seen if you want relative quiet then visit during a week day.

The mountains on this part of the island are the most spectacular and include the highest at Cuber which is Puig Major at 1,447m, with others such as Masanella at 1,352m and Es Tossa at 1.047m which are equally impressive. They look even more impressive during the winter months when they often have snow on their peaks. The reservoir itself is very large. It is fed by the Torrente de Balganac and holds good species of birds.

After the Km4 marker, keep a look above the ridge to your left for both light phase and dark phase Booted Eagles. Once you leave the long straight road and begin the uphill drive you will start to see Hoopoe, Chaffinch, Great Tit and Wren. Any roadside stops amongst the pines will give you a chance of Wryneck, Firecrest and Common Crossbill. After about 50m past the Km25 marker there is a nice restaurant particularly if you want to stop on the way back. After Km26 there is a small pull in at a 'mirador' (view point). There are excellent views into the deep valley deep below and raptors are always possible. There is a small shop built into the rock face here which is usually open and offers ice cream and cold drinks. The rocks around here regularly have a pair of Blue Rock Thrushes amongst them.

Eventually you drive into a long tunnel (use your lights) and immediately as you exit the tunnel pull into the lay by on the left. Blue Rock Thrush will be on the ridge behind you. This reservoir is Embalse de Gorg Blau which was created by seasonal torrents over millions of years. Apart from Yellow-legged Gulls which are always present keep a look out for Osprey which feed here. Continuing along, the road climbs uphill again with several twisting bends. After Km33 you will notice a large gravel car park on your left. Ignore this one and continue around two more bends until you reach a small car park also on the left with a metal gate across a tarmac track. The turning is quite sharp and be aware of drivers approaching behind you.

Park in here, (which is the entrance to Embalse de Cuber – Cuber Reservoir). **(1)** This small car park tends to fill up by mid-morning so you may need to drive back the short distance to the larger car park you just passed. There is a circular route around the reservoir itself. The views and the ridges are breathtaking. The mountain to your right with the military installation on the top is the highest in Mallorca Puig Major (1,447m). By 9am the early morning thermals will already be starting to rise and raptors will be beginning to take advantage of this. Eleven species of raptor are possible here during the summer months including Black Vulture, Egyptian Vulture (and as of December 2008 - Griffon Vulture as well), Eleonora's Falcon, Peregrine Falcon, Booted Eagle (both light and dark phase birds), Red Kite, Black Kite, Kestrel, Hobby and Osprey. **Note:** Previously there was a single Griffon Vulture which roamed along the mountain ridges of the north but on a visit in December 2008 I saw a group of seventeen circling. Again in May 2009 there were still small groups of Griffon's present indicating that perhaps they are staying in this mountain region throughout the year. During a warm day in May 2000 I watched a Golden Eagle flying through. The light was streaming through its wings and it looked absolutely stunning.

Walking in through the gate next to the main gate which usually has around ten or so padlocks on it immediately start checking above the ridges for Black Vulture and raptors. They particularly favour the ridge which runs towards Puig Major. Keep to the tarmac path. The vegetation and the short pines along the left of the path is a good spot for Spectacled Warbler which breed here during the summer. Cirl Bunting and Sub-alpine Warbler can also be found in this area. Some of the habitats the Spectacled Warbler favours have been reduced elsewhere on the island due to tree planting schemes but they have a good foothold at Cuber especially now that young trees have been re-planted across the lower hillsides. Nightingale will also be around this spot. The high ridge to your left is the favoured spot for Cuckoo **(2)**. Stop here and take some time to scan the bushes and vegetation for warblers.

You continue along the path in the direction of the dam scanning amongst the shorter vegetation on your right. Northern Wheatear, Stonechat, Tawny Pipit, Cirl Bunting, Whinchat, wagtails and pipits can all be found around here. You will notice a 'helipad'. During May 1999 I had excellent views of a male Black-eared Wheatear feeding here. Yellow-legged Gulls are always on the reservoir and occasionally Eleonora's Falcons come down to the water's edge to drink. Osprey regularly hunt for the numerous fish to be found in the water and if they don't consume them at the waters edge (as I have seen on numerous occasions) they will fly across to the small pylons and perch on the top of these to enjoy their catch.

(3) The Dam. Stop here and scan below. Crag Martins breed under the dam and Nightingale, Firecrest and warblers feed in the bushes below and on the banks. Cirl Bunting and Serin are regular here and can be easier to watch as you are looking down onto them for a change. Marsh Frog can be heard noisily calling in the stream below as can Mallorcan Midwife Toad – both of which can be seen with patience especially where the water collects below by a small stream.

Just after you walk over the dam and go up a gentle slope you come to a quarry (4) on your left. It is not a very noticeable quarry but it is directly opposite where the path widens for a while. This is a regular spot for Rock Thrush which breeds in this area. They can be found here from May to around September (patience is usually required however to see them).

A little further along the path you reach a notice board. Cross over the wooden stile (or through the adjacent metal gate) and head down to a stone building. There is a picnic bench here. It's a nice spot to have a break and scan the ridges. Linnet, Stonechat and Cirl Bunting are regular at this spot. Tawny Pipits will be displaying here during early May and offer excellent close views especially in the open scrub around the notice board by the main track. The ridges up to the left of the path here are the favourite for Red Kite and Black Kite.

As you cross over a small stream with stepping stones (5) check behind you up-stream for Grey Wagtails. This is the Torrente de Baranc stream which feeds the reservoir. Once you cross onto a wide dust track keep an eye on the ridge to your left. Keep scanning above the whole length of this ridge as you walk as Black Vulture, Griffon Vulture and Booted Eagle will be guaranteed. Yellow-legged Gulls are always on the rock faces here calling noisily. Kestrel and Peregrine

Falcon are found along the walls of these ridges also.

There are electricity poles running along the left hand side of this path. These are a regular resting and feeding place for Osprey. On one such pylon in December 2005 I had good close views of a male Alpine Accentor which winters in this area. The Cork Oaks and other trees on your left are alive with warblers such as Blackcap, Willow Warbler, Garden Warbler, Common Whitethroat and Chiffchaff with Common Redstart, Cirl Bunting, Firecrest and Nightingale also common.

The reservoir is now on your right. Cormorants are usually present in small numbers. The edge of the water regularly has one or two Common Sandpipers feeding along it. They continually fly away along the waters edge as you proceed up the path. There are plenty of goats and sheep along here each one with a small bell around its neck adding a different but subtle noise to the landscape.

Eventually you reach a small concrete walkway over an inlet **(6)** with a concrete water system running underneath which also feeds the reservoir. Common Sandpiper and Grey Wagtail are regular in the small pools here. As you continue along the dirt track leading back towards the car park check the bushes to your left. Firecrest are guaranteed to be feeding in these. I would allow at least three to four hours to complete this walk as there can be plenty of stopping to look at birds. The whole walk is flat and is approximately two and a half miles around and definitely worth one or more visits during a stay on the island.

Winter birding: Being summer visitors Eleonora's Falcon, Nightingale, Tawny Pipit, Rock Thrush and Spectacled Warbler will have gone but most of the birds mentioned above should be present. The only warblers likely to be around are Chiffchaffs. Black Vulture, Egyptian Vulture, Griffon Vulture, Booted Eagle and Red Kite will still be present. Firecrest will be in the bushes and Cirl Bunting will be evident. Common Sandpiper can still be found as can Grey Wagtail. Water Pipit will be present now in low numbers. Alpine Accentor is of course possible during the winter.

At any time of the year after completing this walk you can drive along on the main road down to Soller. The name is Arabic (*Sullier*), meaning '*golden bowl*', probably relating to the many orange groves to be found here. This is a large and lovely town with a pleasant square offering coffee, beers and meals. There are numerous pay and display car parks in the town all reasonably priced. You can catch a tram from here and ride down to Port de Soller which is equally pleasant.

The Trams are old stock from San Francisco during the 1930s and can be boarded at the old station just up from the main square in Soller. If you want a little break from birding for a few hours then this is a pleasant alternative. You can also take a tram ride down to Palma in the south... well recommended!

Lluc Monastery

If however you decide to head back towards Puerto Pollensa then a stop off along the return journey at Lluc Monastery is highly recommended. This is an 11th Century Monastery which is still occupied today. There is a lovely coffee shop and bar there with hot and cold snacks also available, a nice gift shop toilet facilities and of course stunning architecture and amazing history.

As you drive into the large car park just past the Monastery entrance (free parking) continue up to the top of this car park. To your left is a lane with a cattle grid. This area is good for Pied Flycatcher, Firecrest, Nightingale, Hoopoe and warblers. Do not venture past the cattle grid as the road goes on for some time but keep an eye open for Wryneck which favours this area. There are usually a few dogs tied up which bark at your presence but these are not really a problem. Common Crossbills can be found in the tall trees and occasionally Golden Oriole can be seen. Park up in the lower part of the car park and walk in to the Monastery which is well worth a little look around inside. There is a circular walk adjacent to the bar and restaurant accessed at the stone steps. This is a pleasant walk underneath trees which are excellent for Chiffchaff, Willow Warbler, Blackcap, Garden Warbler and Firecrest. The walk is also one of the best during late April and May to watch Nightingales chasing each other in the open. There are some amazing views over the almond and olive groves in the valley below from the top of the path. If the weather is particularly hot this is also a nice walk as you are sheltered from the heat by the trees.

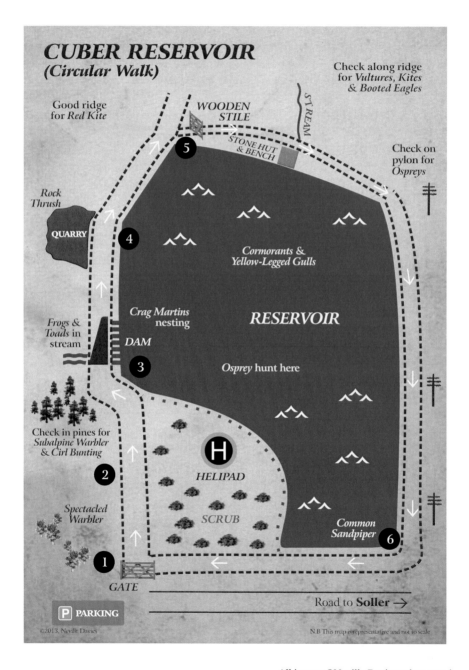

CUBER RESERVOIR
(Circular Walk)

Check along ridge
for *Vultures, Kites*
& Booted Eagles

Good ridge
for *Red Kite*

WOODEN
STILE

STREAM

STONE HUT
& BENCH

5

Check on
pylon for
Ospreys

Rock
Thrush

QUARRY

4

Cormorants &
Yellow-Legged Gulls

Crag Martins
nesting

Frogs &
Toads in
stream

DAM

RESERVOIR

3

Osprey hunt here

Check in pines for
Subalpine Warbler
& Cirl Bunting

H

2

HELIPAD

Spectacled
Warbler

SCRUB

Common
Sandpiper

6

1

GATE

Road to **Soller** →

P PARKING

©2013, Neville Davies

N.B This map is representative and not to scale

All images ©Neville Davies unless stated

SITE 5: CAP DE FORMENTOR and CASES VELLES

Head out of Puerto Pollensa town on the MA-2210 road and follow the brown signs for Formentor. By the military base on the right the road bends around slightly left. Do not stop by the entrance of the military site. Continue to the top of this road where you will see a small roundabout. Before turning right at this roundabout onto the Formentor road itself drive straight across and park by a metal gate with wire meshing across it. This is the entrance to Albercutz Farm **(1)**. Beyond the gate is a private road so viewing is restricted from the gate itself. However the scrub beyond is good for warblers, Woodchat Shrike and Red-legged Partridge and is also a regular spot for Black Kites feeding. The valleys from here all the way to the point at Formentor are a main migratory route for birds entering and leaving the island. Golden Oriole, Northern Wheatear, finches and Hoopoe can be seen from here as well.

Continuing on the main Formentor road you begin to climb up twisting roads with hairpin bends. Along this section of road on the second sharp bend after Alburcutz Farm is a large gate with a wall either side. I have seen Barn Owl sitting on this wall during night drives here on numerous occasions. After a little drive you come to Mirador La Creveta (known simply as Mirador) after the Km5 marker. Park in here **(2)**. There is stunning scenery here and some great birds on offer. Aim to be here early before the coaches arrive with hordes of tourists usually around 9.30am onwards. A concrete path and steps (which have no handrails) leads up to the viewing area. There are spectacular views out over the Mediterranean Sea where Yellow-legged Gulls are plentiful. Look for Blue Rock Thrush, Kestrel, Peregrine Falcon and Crag Martins along the cliffs. There is a small colony of Pallid Swifts which breed here and Alpine Swift can occasionally be seen. Eleonora's Falcons breed on the sheer cliffs around here. Behind you there is another road which leads up to a tall stone tower. Ignore this one for now as it can be visited on the return journey.

Driving on along the twisting roads you eventually come to a fork in the road. Straight on takes you up the Hotel Formentor with its private beach. There is a car park and a short walk which takes you to a lovely beach and a modern cafe prior to the hotel itself. There are also boat trips from here to Puerto Pollensa. I tend to follow the road around to the left and continue on through the pine forests and head for Formentor. The road here straightens out for a while through an avenue of pines. Night drives along this road have given me Nightjar and Pine Martins on the roadside.

Immediately after the Km11 marker post pull onto a small grass area on the left next to a wall. This is Cases Velles **(3)** and one of the best migration spots on the island. It is worth spending some time here as the bird species can change rather quickly as birds pass through. Unless you stay at the luxurious Formentor Hotel then access into the pine forests is forbidden. Do not be tempted to climb the fences and walk in. The Guardia Civil will be called and you will be escorted out. This is not from personal experience but I have seen several tempted birdwatchers spend some time explaining why they are in a private area. However viewing from the roadside is allowed and highly recommended.

Once you park up and exit your vehicle the first calls you normally hear are the '*chip chip*' calls of Common Crossbills. These are a sub-species, *balearica*, and have a Catalan name of '*trencapinyons*' which means pine nut cracker. They feed amongst the pines on the abundance of cones and offer excellent views. Serin and Firecrest will also be present. The resident Peacock in the large house can be very vocal too. The fig and almond trees in the fields on both sides of the road are excellent for migrants and can include Spotted Flycatcher and Pied Flycatcher in good numbers, Common Redstart, Chiffchaff, Willow Warbler, Blackcap, Common Whitethroat, Northern Wheatear and Whinchat with various finches and buntings mixed in too. Ortolan Bunting can be fairly regular. Red-throated Pipit and Olive-backed Pipit have both been recorded here.

Check along the telephone wires and poles in the right hand field for Kestrel, Woodpigeon, Turtle Dove, Hoopoe and occasionally Roller. Golden Oriole is likely occasionally perched up on the wires but also in the foliage of the groves where they can take some spotting. I found a male Collard Flycatcher here in 2006 which was a lovely surprise. The Bramble bushes and scrub on the roadside alongside the walls are excellent for Sardinian Warbler. It really is worth a good look as this site which can be alive with birds and this can change literally by the hour.

Raptors especially Peregrine Falcon and Booted Eagle will be found above the ridges with Ravens mixed in enjoying the same warm thermals. Walk up the road a short way to the two gates which are opposite each other. Serin and Firecrest will be seen in the pines around here and if any pools are visible on the woodland floor from the roadside then it is possible you may see Crossbills coming to them to drink. Their diet consists of pine seeds which can make them quite thirsty. This is also a particularly good spot during an evening drive to see Scops Owl in the trees near to these gates. You will certainly hear several males calling. I have mimicked their call and had them flying overhead on several occasions.

Driving on will soon bring you to a tunnel. There is a pull in with space for about two cars on the left immediately as you exit the tunnel. Park here if there is room and look down at the water below - it is the most stunning turquoise colour. Please take care however it is a long way down. The views here are stunning and the high ridge behind you can be good for Egyptian Vulture, Booted Eagle and Peregrine Falcon.

Continue driving until eventually you reach the lighthouse itself **(4)** at Cap de Formentor. There is parking available but will fill up when the coaches and visitors arrive by mid-morning. However more parking spaces have been created so linger around and a space will become available. There is a lovely coffee shop inside the lighthouse which offers a range of hot and cold snacks and is a good place to sit on the balcony and scan out to sea for both Balearic and Cory's Shearwaters which can be found offshore here. Ibiza can be seen from here on a clear day. There are high ridges here including Es Fumat at 334m. Offshore migrants can also include Black Stork, White Stork and Gannet. Blue Rock Thrush, Eleonora's Falcon and Crag Martin all breed on the cliffs here.

Adjacent to the toilets is a good scrub area with a scattering of erect and fallen pine trees. Spend some time looking here as it can be alive with migrants. If (as I have done) there is a heavy rain fall drive up to the lighthouse and wait for the rain to stop. These bushes are a haven for migrants grounded by the heavy rain. Once the rain eases the vegetation gives way to migrants sometimes in high numbers and can include Chiffchaff, Wood Warbler, Willow Warbler, Common Whitethroat, Blackcap, Garden Warbler, Common Redstart, Northern Wheatear, Whinchat, Pied Flycatcher and Spotted Flycatcher amongst others.

The Balearic Shearwaters are of particular interest to the birdwatcher here as they are amongst the third rarest species with a world population of around only 3,000 pairs. They breed between February and June raising only one chick. Scan out towards the horizon with a telescope to improve your chances of seeing them.
Enjoy the stunning views in every direction. The distant ridge looking away from the lighthouse has a pair of Blue Rock Thrush which hold territory here. From the lighthouse itself you will be looking out towards the neighbouring islands of Ibiza and Menorca. The sea is vast so take some time to look for Gannets which feed

offshore. Cory's Shearwaters will be present in small numbers usually far out so a telescope is helpful in spotting them. They bob up and down as they fly close to the water. Also mixed in are the rarer Balearic Shearwaters – a target species.

On the return route retracing your steps stop again at Cases Velles to see what new migrants may have turned up. Back at the Mirador (point 2) take the road up to your left. Follow a steep road up to the large Moorish watch tower - Talaca de Albercutz. The road is a bit narrow in places and there is a small turning circle and limited parking after you pass the derelict buildings on your right although traffic up to here is generally light especially during the afternoon. The Moorish Tower itself was used during World War II as a look out for advancing German fighters. The ceiling had pictures of German aircraft drawn onto it for identification purposes. Sadly these have now been plastered over as part of the upkeep of the tower at the time of my last visit. There are a series of steel steps leading up inside the tower if one wants to have a look inside.

The views from the cliffs are spectacular and you can look down onto the fields at Cases Velles and the Formentor Hotel. The scrub area is excellent for warblers but during migration time in April and May raptor passage can also be good here. During a particularly warm May in 2009 whilst sat next to the tower looking out at sea I noticed a group of twenty one large birds coming up the ridge towards me from the open sea. As they got closer I could see they were raptors. They slowly made their way past me to within about thirty feet. I counted eighteen Honey Buzzards and three Black Kites, a magnificent site which will stay with me forever. This is one of the magical things about the bird life in Mallorca; you never know what will turn up and where?

Winter birding: During the whole drive from points 1 to 3 (especially) the amount of Black Redstarts and Chiffchaffs will be impressive. Blue Rock Thrush, Sardinian Warbler, Kestrel, Peregrine Falcon and Yellow-legged Gulls will be present. Crossbills, Firecrest, Serins, Chaffinch and Woodpigeons will all be at Cases Velles, and it is still well worth a stop there. Unless you particularly want to drive up to the lighthouse (bear in mind that the summer visitors will be gone) then turn back and use the time to visit another site. The lighthouse restaurant is open during the winter but times may vary.

Note: Due to the distances involved and complexity of this route, there is no site map available. Please refer to the main body text for guidance.

SITE 5: SALINAS DE LEVANTE - THE SALT PANS

This site is also known as Salobrar de Campos but to most birdwatchers it is simply known as the Salt Pans. Being in the south of the island this will be the furthest site away from Puerto Pollensa. It is however well recommended that you pay a visit here as the birding is excellent. It is a pleasant drive through a mixture of open countryside towns and villages. Start out early for this journey as there is a chance you may miss or take a few wrong turns especially in Manacor and Felanitx. In fact my last visit was the first time I have ever completed the journey without any mistakes. It all adds to the fun.

To reach the Salt Pans, drive towards Alcudia on the MA-2200 road and join the MA-12 sign-posted for Arta. From here join the MA-15 for Manacor. Head into the town itself (world famous for its pearls) and join the MA-14 to Felanitx. Go through here and stay on the MA-14 road into Santanyi. This is where directions can be a bit confusing, but stick with it as you are not far from the Salt Pans now.

Join the MA-6100 to the small village of Llombards and then onto Ses Salines where you join the MA-6101. Drive until you see the MA-6040 road where you turn left. After a short drive (heading in the direction of Colnia Sant Jordi) you will see a large sign on your right '*Banys de la Font Santa*'. Turn in here and park down by the entrance of a hotel where there is ample parking space outside. Don't worry if you miss the turn onto this side road there are plenty of turning places.

During the summer months if you lke you can have a nice cup of coffee or a beer at the hotel either inside or in the garden at the front of the hotel. This is quite pleasant before beginning the walk.

(1) At the entrance of the hotel where you have parked (please take care not to block the gates) follow a noticeable rough track on your right which runs alongside open fields on both sides of the track. Scan here for pipits, buntings, Thekla Lark and Hoopoe. Marsh Harrier can be seen hunting here and Quail is possible. These fields can sometimes be alive with wagtails, pipits and buntings, so it is worth scanning through them for possible rarities.

When you reach the end of this track before it bears to the left have a look over the small lagoon directly in front of you **(2)**. This is a good area for ducks and waders in spring and summer and can include (when the water level is high) Black-winged Stilt, Bar-tailed Godwit and Marsh Sandpiper on passage with Purple Heron likely. When the water level is lower the smaller waders such as Little Stints (check also for Temincks Stint), Common Redshank, Common Sandpiper and Kentish Plovers can be found along with Mallard and other ducks. Harriers can be seen anywhere from here together with Booted Eagle, Peregrine Falcon, Kestrel, Osprey and occasionally Hobby.

(3) Take the left path past three tall Palm trees and follow this to where it bends slightly around to the right. The scrub here is good for warblers such as Fan-tailed and Sardinian Warbler and it was amongst the vegetation here in December 2005 I watched a White-spotted Bluethroat feeding. There are some lagoons on the left here which are nearly always dry. Check this area for Collard Pratincole which particularly like this spot, Kentish Plover, Little Ringed Plover and Ringed Plover. Other waders on passage are likely and Stone Curlew is regularly seen feeding here.

(4) Now you are on a long straight path with numerous lagoons on either side. This area can be very damp for about a hundred yards or so especially during the winter months so you may find yourself walking in and out of the short vegetation alongside the path for a while to avoid the puddles. Persevere however as the birding here really is spectacular. The path runs alongside a small water pumping building on the left. There are a series of lagoons on both sides of the path with varying depths of water which hold a good number of species.

Take time to scan each lagoon on both sides for Whiskered Tern and Little Tern, Kentish Plover, Little Egret, Purple Heron, Bar-tailed Godwit, Wood Sandpiper, Curlew Sandpiper, Black-winged Stilt, Little Stint, (possible Teminck's Stint), Dunlin and Common Redshank amongst others. Water Rail can be heard and sometimes seen. I watched a Bean Goose feeding here in 2008 which was a nice surprise. These lagoons can be packed with waders especially during the spring and summer months when migration is in full swing.

Spring passage may see White Stork and Spoonbill. Greater Flamingo is likely to be feeding in the deeper lagoons usually on the left side of the path. From time to time everything flies up from the lagoons. This usually signifies a raptor so look for Booted Eagle, Peregrine Falcon, Kestrel and Osprey which are common hunters here. The telegraph wires are regularly used for perching by Stonechat,

Whinchat, Spotted Flycatcher and Woodchat Shrike. This can be a good spot for Red-footed Falcons which regularly rest along the wires when on migration.

The low scrub is very thick on both sides of the track so check on the tops for wagtail species such as the blue-headed iberiae and occasional *flavissima* races. Fan-tailed Warblers are always visible amongst or above the scrub and Chiffchaffs are busy eating insects from within. Stonechats are always present on top of the scrub.

When you reach the second of the green camouflaged pump houses **(5)** the track ends. It is private property past this point but do take advantage to scan over the lagoons to the left. Cetti's Warblers are common around here and usually show quite well and the open muddy area in front of you which is normally dry can hold Short-toed Lark and Thekla Larks.

You will notice the telegraph poles going away from you here into the distance on your left. Carefully check along the wires and on the posts as the Osprey favours these particular posts to scan the lagoons before flying off to hunt fish. Red-footed Falcons perch along these wirres when on migration. This is also a good area in and around the lagoons for tern species such as Gull-billed Tern (on migration), Little Tern, Whiskered Tern, Black Tern and White-winged Black Tern. Also possible as vagrants are Roseate Terns. Caspian Tern and Lesser-crested Tern have also been recorded here. It really is a fantastic area for birds with plenty of surprises.

There is a large amount of bare bushes around here which hold Bee Eaters amongst other species. Check amongst these bushes for warblers. As you walk back to point 1 it is worth re-checking what is on the lagoons as with migration under full swing there may well be something new and of course you will now be scanning from a different direction.

Note: Due to this being a salt area the sun can be reflected quite strongly from the ground. You may find you need to wear sunglasses or at least have a hat that shades the eyes. Sun tan lotion and mosquito repellent are advised on this walk. Mosquitoes are plentiful in the water areas and although they don't normally pose a problem a bite can be irritating. It is however a wonderful birding site and well worth the drive.

During a week's stay I visit this site at least twice as the birding is that good! The walk should take you up to lunch time (from the early morning). However one could quite easily spend the whole day here if time allowed. After visiting the Salt Pans I tend to drive onto Colonia Sant Jordi and have some lunch before continuing onto the next site of Es Trenc which is close by.

Winter birding: Whenever I visit the island during the winter I always put a visit in to the Salt Pans as the birding is still very rewarding. Along the rough track at point 1 check the field on the right. Skylarks can be found wintering here in large numbers with occasional Thekla Lark and Red Legged Partridges present. The water area at point 2 is particularly good for Black-winged Stilt, Little Stint (along the shallow edges), Common Redshank, Green Sandpiper, Common Sandpiper, Mallard, Coot, Shoveler, Wigeon, Teal and Grey Heron.

Check the scrub from the vicinity of the three pine trees to the end of the main track for Fan-tailed Warbler, Stonechat, Chiffchaff and Grey Wagtail. During December 2007 I had excellent views of a White-spotted Bluethroat in the scrub near to the three pines. Check the muddy area on the left for Kentish Plover and Ringed Plover, Little Stint, Curlew Sandpiper and White Wagtails. As you walk down the long straight path past the lagoons check each one for Water Rail, Water Pipit and waders including Curlew, Common Snipe, Jack Snipe, Bar-tailed Godwit, Dunlin, Golden Plover and Lapwing. Other wader species may also be present. During December 2008 a single Bean Goose was mixed in with the waders here. The deeper lagoons to your left hold Greater Flamingo', Little Egret, occasionally Great White Egret, Grey Heron and Cormorants feeding . Raptors can be numerous and include Booted Eagle, Kestrel and Peregrine Falcon. Osprey and Marsh Harriers are always present.

Es Trenc

Once you have returned to your vehicle by the hotel drive up to the main road and take a right turn. After a short distance you will see another right turn signposted Es Trenc. Turn in here and follow the road until you are alongside the mounds of salt and the machinery workings on the right **(1)**. This site is well worth a visit and offers a different view over the Salt Pans. There are small pull-ins along the road which offers good views over the lagoons. New signs have been erected all along this stretch of road warning of vehicles being towed away if left there. So if you do view from the roadside stay with your vehicle.

Check the lagoons for Common Shelduck, Mallard, Moorhen, Avocet (which can be in large numbers), Kentish Plover, Ringed Plover, Little Ringed Plover, Curlew Sandpiper, Dunlin, Little Stint (checking through these for the occasional Teminck's Stints with their yellowish tinged legs), Collard Pratincole, Bar-tailed Godwit, Wood Sandpiper and terns such as Whiskered Tern and Little Tern. Blue-headed Wagtails (*flava*) can be found feeding on the mud.

(2) Drive a little further along until you see a noticeably open section of grass fields on the left. During 2011 there were no signs present stating that vehicles were not to be left here. However please check this before you park up. Park here and take a walk towards the pine trees. Go slightly right of these and over a low block wall. Explore this area before and beyond the wall in the open scrubby area with a raised sandy bank in the foreground. This is an excellent spot for species such as Hoopoe, Thekla Lark, Corn Bunting, Bee Eater, Spotted Flycatcher, Pied Flycatcher, Common Redstart, Whinchat, Stonechat, Linnet, Tawny Pipit, Woodchat Shrike, Serin and Nightingale. Please be cautious here as Stone Curlew sometimes nests on the ground around here. If you see any particularly in flight then they may well be nesting and alarmed at your presence so please return to the roadside and scan from there. This area is also good for large clumps of bright red Hottontot Fig growing.

Returning to the vehicle continue driving slowly checking the water areas to your right. After a little while you will notice a large open expanse of green on your left **(3)** leading away to some trees. This area can be good for Red-footed Falcon and Kestrel. During May 2007 the group I was leading here had excellent views of a Bonelli's Eagle in this area. Red-legged Partridges can be seen here also.

Continue on along the road which leads into the pine wood area. This eventually leads to a car park. I turn around in here and slowly continue back. The car park (which incurs a fee) is for the nearby Es Trenc nudist beach. The pine area itself is good for Serin, Nightingale, Firecrest and sometimes Bonelli's Warbler.

Winter birding: The lagoons will be full of Dunlin, Little Stint and other waders feeding with good numbers of Common Shelduck on the far banks. Marsh Harriers will be present. In the open scrub area **(point 2)**, look for Mistle Thrush, Blackbird, Song Thrush, Sardinian Warbler, Chiffchaff and Black Redstart, finches and White Wagtails. Common Starlings are usually present in good numbers.

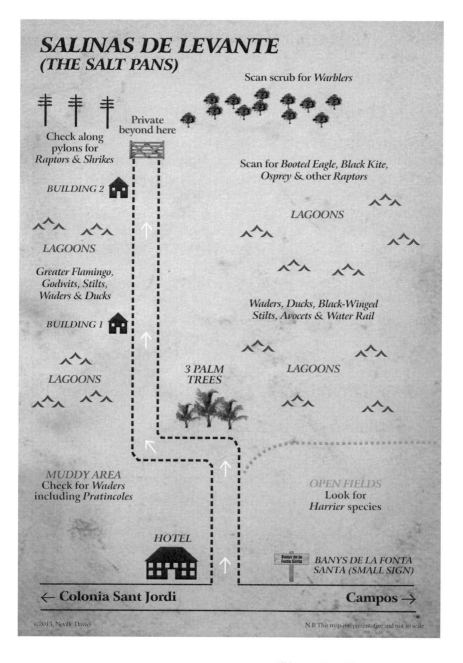

All images ©Neville Davies unless stated

Cap de ses Salines

After a visit to the Salt Pans and Es Trenc I used to take the short drive down to Colnia Sant Jordi to do some birdwatching there. However, in recent years I have found this not to be very good for birds and after a bit of experimenting I came across the nearby Far de Cap Selines which has proved to be more worthwhile bird wise.

Off the main road, take the MA-6110 road. It is a lovely drive down to the lighthouse with Red-legged Partridges to be found in the fields. Once you reach where the road ends park up and walk along the path adjacent to the wall by the lighthouse.

Check the scrub within the lighthouse grounds from the wall for warblers and particularly along the coastal area too. Dartford Warbler is possible as is Balearic Warbler in the thick scrub. Short-toed Larks can be found around the beach area and Audouin's Gulls are usually present too. There is a record for Iberia's second Bar-tailed Desert Lark from here (*Hearl, Graham*). As you walk along the left hand path (the lighthouse will be on your left) keep an eye open for both Thekla Lark and Tawny Pipit which favour the habitat here.

There are regular fishing trawlers off shore here so check amongst the many Yellow-legged Gulls which will be following behind the boats for other species mixed in. Cory's and Balearic Shearwater are usually present either behind the trawlers or further out on the horizon. However during bad weather both these species can be closer in offering good views as they fly past.

Note: See Castle de Santuri as a site to visit on the return to Puerto Pollensa.

ADDITIONAL SITES

Puerto Pollensa back roads and Llenaire Road (Bee Hive Lane)
Cala San Vicente
Puerto Pollensa Inlet
Puerto Pollensa Harbour and Beach
Puerto Pollensa Breakwaters
Puerto Pollensa town - Scops Owl site
Ulls de Rec (Smelly River)
Ternells Valley
Castel de Santuri
Porto Colom
Arta Mountains

The main sites as covered in part three can all be comfortably completed during a week's stay. There are of course options open such as re-visiting a particular site especially if one is keen to see a species missed on the first site visit. The following section is aimed at those who are staying for more than a week and wish to explore some lesser known but good birding sites. Please bear in mind that all of these sites except the last three sites can be covered during a pre-breakfast visit as I generally tend to do.

The light does not disappear until around 8.35pm in the summer so there is plenty of time for a whole day's birding. Light levels are strong giving the birds an overall cleaner brighter looking appearance. Sites further afield such as Porto Colom and Arta are best visited if you are staying over a week as they are large areas and you could easily spend a whole day in the mountains exploring the many tracks and roads. Castle de Santuri however is a nice drive in itself and can be rewarding bird wise. It can be visited on a return trip from Es Trenc and the Salt Pans as it is situated just outside of Santanyi on the way back to Puerto Pollensa.

Puerto Pollensa Back Roads and Llenaire Road (Bee Hive Lane)

Being on the edges or close proximity to Puerto Pollensa the back roads are great for exploring before breakfast or during the late afternoon especially as the weather can be slightly cooler during these times. You will be taking a lot of left and right turns as you go and along with the commoner species these sites can be worthwhile for additional species. By visiting these back roads I have seen several interesting birds such as Eurasian Bittern, Great White Egret, Red-footed Falcon and Roller to name a few. The following routes are all accessed from the coast road leading out to Puerto Pollensa towards Alcudia.

1. As you leave Puerto Pollensa on the coast road heading towards Alcudia you leave the main part of the town and start to look for Bar Llenaire which will be on your right. Continue past Bar llenaire for about 300m. Turn in right by the Can Cuarassa restaurant and follow the gravel road to the end. Turn left. This is an excellent area for close views of Nightingales which tend to be everywhere. Cetti's Warbler will be present. Take the next right onto a rough track (which is bumpy but driveable) and scan this area for harrier species which pass through on migration. I have seen Montagu's Harrier here and Marsh Harriers are regular. Red-footed Falcon, hunt over the open fields here. Blue-headed Wagtail, Corn Bunting and Fan-tailed Warbler are present in good numbers. There are damp areas around the fields so look for Purple Heron, Squacco Heron, Little Egret and waders. Check along the wires for Kestrel, Woodchat Shrike and Bee Eaters. Roller is possible here on migration.

This road eventually leads onto a grey coloured stone dust track. Follow this around to the left where the track then forks. Take a left and scan the olive groves to your left for Golden Oriole, Woodchat Shrike, Roller and Wryneck. At the stop sign, turn left and follow this road back to the coast road which will take you back to Puerto Pollensa.

2. When leaving Puerto Pollensa and heading along the coast road towards Alcudia look for a right turn signposted Cami Volantina. Turn in here and follow the road until you reach a bend where there is a safety barrier. There is a small pull-in here for one vehicle, park here. The river on your right has extensive vegetation which is particularly good for a variety for warbler species. Night Heron, Moorhen, Coot, Little Egret, Mallard and Cormorant can all be found here. Wagtails regularly feed on the exposed mud. Further along at the end of the hedge you can stop alongside the river to scan back up along the river. The habitat here looks ideal for crake species so it is well worth keeping an eye out.

Walk back to the vehicle and slowly continue along this road in the direction your vehicle is facing. The open field on the left regularly has Cattle Egret in good numbers feeding amongst the sheep and cattle. They can be quite comical as they will regularly perch up on the backs of the animals. A little further on you will have some more open views of the river. Follow the road around several bends. Check along the telephone wires for Roller and Turtle Dove both of which stop and rest on these wires during migration. I have had some great views of Roller in this particular area.

Turn right at the stop sign and bridge. Pheasants can be seen around here. You are now on what is known by birders as **'Beehive Lane'** in reference to the once many hives that could be found here. There are extensive fig, almond and olive groves here so spend some time to look for key species such as Golden Oriole, Wryneck, Woodchat Shrike, Hoopoe, Roller other migrants and warblers. It is worth parking up and walking alongside the wall listening out for any calls and scanning the groves from both sides of the road. Be careful of through traffic on this road though.

Back at your vehicle head to the stop sign near a bridge and continue on to the junction. Turn to head towards Puerto Pollensa. Follow the road until you reach another stop sign. Take a left then the next right and go over the small bridge. There is a nice little stream running along the left hand side and is good for close views of Night Heron and Nightingales in the thick vegetation.

At the next junction take a left turn signposted Alcudia. This is a good area for Marsh Harrier (Hen Harriers and Skylarks in winter) Hoopoe and Corn Buntings. Continue on this road for about half a mile. The landscape opens up again and you will notice a large area of water away to your left. Park here as this is a good spot for water species. Yellow-legged Gull and Whiskered Tern can be seen. I have seen Greater Flamingo and Eurasian Bittern here on numerous occasions. Ducks can be found especially during the winter and occasionally Glossy Ibis can be seen. There is a good expanse of water here so take some time to scan it with a telescope and check the vegetation beyond. During several of my last visits I have been having good sightings of Osprey from here usually perched up on the low posts in the water and occasionally eating a fish.

Continue on the road heading for Alcudia. When you reach the main road turn left and follow the sign for Puerto Pollensa which takes you back onto the coast road and towards the town.

Cala San Vicente

This is a beautiful town nestled in a deep valley with the Serra de Sant Vicente ridges overlooking the area. The town itself is set on the coast in a stunning area. Not surprising then that the late Sir Harry Secombe owned a home here and Cilla Black also has a residence. You will notice brown signs on the right hand side as you drive in for some caves which are funeral caves from the Meditterranean Bronze Age and are believed to be around 3,500 years old adding some great history along with the wonderful birds in the area.

Take the MA-2203 road from Puerto Pollensa (not the coast road) towards Soller. Drive through the roundabout adjacent to the Habitat Apartments and continue past the turning for Gotmar and along the straight road. Once on this road keep an eye out for Kestrel, Collard Dove, House Sparrow, Stonechat and Bee Eaters.

The turning for Cala San Vicente will be on your right. Drive slowly as this is a very pleasant area with lovely views and plenty of birds. This whole area can be particularly good at night for Scops Owl and the occasional Barn Owl and Tawny Owl.

After the Km2 marker look for a brown sign on the right marked Cami de Can Botana. Turn in here and park under the pine trees. Walk down the path to where the landscape opens on your right so that you're looking down a long straight field with a small stream running alongside. Bonelli's Warbler is possible here as is Firecrest, Hoopoe and Nightingale. On one occasion I watched a Montagu's Harrier quartering this particular field. Wryneck and Golden Oriole can be possible here. Greenfinch and Chaffinch are present in good numbers with smaller groups of Common Crossbills and Serin in the pines.

As an alternative in the hot weather or to fill in an afternoons birding you can walk along the path through the gate in front of you and into the main pine area. Keep to the top path for about a mile before reaching the harbour at Cala San Vicente and this is a lovely walk during a hot day where you are sheltered by the pine trees. There is a lot of bird activity within the pines.

Returning to your vehicle turn right and continue towards the town of Cala San Vicente. There are pine forests which can be explored on the left. Drive past the classic car showroom on the right and onto the small car park at the end of the road where it drops down towards the sea. Park here for great views over the sea.

There are some lovely restaurants in this area. The scrub and bushes around here are excellent for warblers such as Willow Warbler, Chiffchaff, Common Whitethroat, Lesser Whitethroat (occasionally), Wood Warbler, Garden Warbler and Blackcap.

Once on the move again drive past the Don Pedro Hotel up to the junction and turn left. Follow the one way road around a few bends and down to the square. Park here and take a look at the stunning turquoise waters. There are several paths leading up onto the pine covered hillside. The most popular one though is accessed back on the road near to the Km55 marker. This is known as *'The Saddle'* at Gommar. One can walk right up and over the Saddle and down the other side where you will see the town of Puerto Pollensa and its harbour in front of you. Raven, Peregrine Falcon, Kestrel, Red-legged Partridge, Sardinian Warbler and scrub warblers are regular as are Booted Eagle and Egyptian Vulture.

For the more adventurous, during the evening you can take the left hand road at the harbour here towards the rough track. This can be followed up to the top. The road however becomes very pot holed but is passable with care. Once at the top keep an eye out for Barn Owls which can be seen here and are usually perched up on a telegraph pole. From here you will be looking down onto the Don Pedro Hotel and during a clear night the sky is absolutely filled with stars. It was during one such evening parked up here that I seen a Genet.

Puerto Pollensa Inlet

There is a large open expanse of water which is tidal fed by the sea known locally as La Goma. As you approach the main part of the town (heading away from the harbour towards Alcudia) look for the river bridge over the water which is running under the main road just up from the shops and bars. Take a left passing Trotters Bar. The owners here love everything to do with the sit-com and even have a sign there saying 'Hookie Street'. Occasionally the three wheeler replica van is there too. Take another left by a large brown wooden building which is a bird and wildlife information centre for the area. Parking is available along the adjacent streets and the lay-by with a full sized elephant outside of a restaurant.

There is an inlet here surrounded by low vegetation which is tidal fed and rises in level several times throughout the day. Little Egret and Common Sandpiper are always present. Swallow, House Martin, Sand Martin and Common Swift aerial feed over the water on the abundance of insects. Purple Heron and Moorhen can be found along the waters edge with warblers in the scrub at the top end. This site looks excellent for crake species so it's always worth having a good look along the pool edges. In the winter look for Grey Heron, Cormorant, Common Sandpiper, Green Sandpiper, Kingfisher, White Wagtail and Chiffchaffs.

Recently a series of boardwalks have been put in place around the inlet with several information boards and benches provided. The walkway now allows the water area to be viewed from different angles. Have a look around inside the information centre too. It is staffed and there are displays and plenty of information. Books and other gifts can be purchased here if the centre is open.

Puerto Pollensa Harbour and Beach

From the main road heading into Puerto Pollensa town there is a lovely sandy beach running alongside the road on your right. During the summer months the beach is well used by tourists but in the less used areas of the beach check any gulls closely. This is an excellent stretch for Audouin's Gull which seems to be quite at home sharing their habitat with the sun lovers. They are a resident breeder with numbers steadily increasing year by year. There is also a narrow but long exposed area of rock just offshore where gulls, Common Terns, (Sandwich Terns in winter) and Shag like to perch. Greater Flamingos occasionally pass in small groups.

Once at the harbour you should have equally good views of the Audouin's Gulls and human activity is a little less here too. There is an avenue of pines to the left of the harbour leading alongside restaurants and bars heading away from the town. House Sparrows use these during the day but a slow walk along here during the evening could reward you with a Scops Owl. In a side street near here in May 2008 whilst sat outside a bar having an evening meal I had a brief view of a Common Dormouse.

Puerto Pollensa Breakwaters

Again on the coast road heading out of Puerto Pollensa towards Alcudia look for a large hotel on your left as you head in the direction of the harbour named *'Hotel Azul'*. This is where the original weekly bird meetings used to take place. The bay across from here has exposed rocks and is a good place to watch Shag perched up. They are the Mediterranean sub-species 'desmarestii'. Sandwich Terns will be present in the winter months. Cormorant and Yellow-legged Gulls are present throughout the year and Audouin's Gulls will be mixed in too. During the winter, the majority of Audouin's Gulls move to the south of the island but there are always several pairs staying along the north coast. Greater Flamingo may be present flying through on migration.

Puerto Pollensa Town – Scops Owl Site

Heading along the coast road towards Alcudia look for a sign on the right for the Guardia Civil, which is adjacent to a group of pine trees with a children's playground. There are several large different coloured industrial waste bins on the side street - park along here. Please be aware that the Guardia Civil is located close by but during April to August there is usually a large group of birders gathered here for the owls in the evening so one doesn't tend to look suspicious with binoculars and cameras. The residents are aware of the owls and the attraction they offer. If however you are the only birdwatchers here during an early evening visit then it may be courteous to let the Guardia Civil know what you are doing in case they get any calls. Take a field guide in with you to show them the owl picture. I have to be honest though I have never had any problems here from anyone and I have visited this location countless times.

Arrive around 8pm during May and June to check amongst the pines for the owls which sometimes roost in the trees. The light will be fading soon after and the owls become vocal before they start flying around. Similarly check the large building on the corner opposite the waste bins. There are a series of ventilation holes on the side of the building and the owls sometimes roost in these too. During one particular evening in May 2003 I watched a Common Swift fly up into one of the holes only to be promptly grabbed by a Scops Owl which was already inside. The owl then descended rapidly towards the ground letting go of the Swift at the last minute. It was an amazing and very unusual site and one I doubt I will ever see again.

Eventually though you will hear the Scops Owls calling from all over the place and you will see several flying back and forth. Check on the telephone wires and on fences in particular. These seem to be the favoured perching spots. Again please be aware that you are in a residential area especially when looking up at any houses for owls. Hotels with bright lights outside attract Scops Owls which feed on moths attracted to the strong lights.

Also situated within the town is the largest hotel on the island – the Pollensa Park. This hotel is quite prominent and has a good selection of mature trees around the grounds mainly Eucalyptus and Poplars. These can be good for roosting Scops Owls. Also here in some years a pair of Ring-necked Parakeets will nest in the hotel grounds. Their presence is usually given away by their raucous call and they can be seen flying around the general area.

Ulls de Rec (Smelly River)

Head south on the coast road out of Puerto Pollenca town. Turn right where it is sign-posted 'Pollenca' and continue for about 2.3km up to a sharp right hand bend. Take the left turn over a Torrente (small stream). This is known as the Smelly River area. The smell can fluctuate in strength depending on the weather but it is worth persevering as the area can be great for birds. These can include Little Bittern, Squacco Heron, Night Heron, Little Egret, Green Sandpiper, Common Sandpiper and other wader species. The surrounding vegetation is good for warblers Nightingales and occasionally Golden Oriole during migration.

Ternells Valley

At one time one could walk up into the stunning valley here, where the thick vegetation was a haven for warblers and many other species. Unfortunately the valley itself is closed to the public. However a drive up to the entrance can be worthwhile if you have a spare hour or so.

To get here take the Puerto Pollensa road from the harbour and head towards old Pollenca. Pass the turning for Cala San Vicente and continue to the roundabout. Go straight through the roundabout on to the Soller road (MA-10). A little further along on your right look for a small brown sign marked Ternells Valley.

Turn in onto the narrow tarmac road which twists around several bends. Sardinian Warblers are always present along the way. Beautiful Borgonvillia hangs over many of the walls and houses adding a splash of deep colour to the scene. A little further along will take you into a narrow gorge. This is the entrance of the valley and you can drive no further once you reach the large wooden gates. However park up and spend some time here. The ridges here peak at 839m.

The river running through the gorge below is the Torrente de Ariant. It has thick scrub along its banks and Cirl Bunting, Nightingale, Firecrest and warblers will be found in the scrub. Wagtail species can be seen amongst the rocks alongside the river. Look above the ridges for Peregrine Falcon, Booted Eagle, Red Kite and occasionally Black Kite. This is also a good spot for Egyptian Vulture. Blue Rock Thrush is present on the walls of the gorge.

Parking spaces are limited and turning the car can be tricky but it is worth a look here and finding a parking space has never been a problem.

Castel de Santuri

This is the site of a 14th Century ruined Arab fortress with commanding views over the olive groves and valleys below. This location can be visited after a trip to the Salt Pans (Salinas de Llevante) as it is on the return trip to Puerto Pollensa. To reach the castle head on the Santanyi road (if you get to Felanitx you've gone too far). Near to the Km1.5 marker look for a brown sign marked Castel de Santuri, turn in here. Follow this narrow road to the castle which is approximately 5.4km.

In the open fields look for Hoopoe, Stone Curlew, Thekla Lark, Red-legged Partridge and Turtle Dove in particular. During one memorable May in 2007 in one of these fields to the left of the road I watched one Hoopoe, one Woodchat Shrike, three male Cirl Buntings, two Sub-alpine Warblers, a pair of Stonechats, one Corn Bunting, two Thekla Larks, four Common Redstarts, seven Red-legged Partridges and a pair of nesting Stone Curlews. What a brilliant morning that was and most of these species are generally present here at all times during the breeding season especially.

The road soon begins to slowly climb up hill to the castle itself. There are numerous parking spaces available once you reach the castle. You do not need to enter the castle which is usually closed anyway to see a good variety of birds. However on the rare occasion it is open for about two Euros each you can enter. It is worth a visit for its historical interests and the 360° views are spectacular. On the steep rock face on which the castle sits look for Crag Martin and Blue Rock Thrush. There is a very small Alpine Swift colony to be found here from about late

April onwards usually of around two breeding pairs. There are steps leading up to the castle entrance with plenty of shrubs and trees where Firecrest, Nightingale and warblers can all be found. Fighting for supremacy still occurs around the castle but thankfully these days only from the Crag Martins and Blue Rock Thrushes jostling for the best rock ledges. The castle is an amazing site built effectively on the edge of a sheer cliff face.

Winter birding: Check the open fields for Thekla Lark, Skylark, Chiffchaff, Robin, Black Redstart, Stone Curlew, Hoopoe, White Wagtail and Starlings. At the castle Blue Rock Thrush can be found on the rock face as can Crag Martin with Firecrest and warblers feeding in the abundant vegetation around

Porto Colom

It is rumoured that Christopher Columbus was born here and no doubt he too would have marvelled at the beautiful landscape and the rugged mountains. This is another good birding area which I visit if staying for more than a week. It is reached by heading to Felanitx and following the signs for Porto Colom. As you drive into Porto Colom you will notice good scrub areas which with a bit of searching you will see Balearic Warbler and Thekla Lark. There has been some development in the area but it is still good for migrants. It is a very pleasant town with a number of paths and birding habitats in and around it. There are open fields ideal for Red-legged Partridge, Thekla Lark, Hoopoe, wagtails and pipits. Skylark can be numerous in winter.

There is a nice walk along the cliff edge as well where migrants such as Whinchat, Common Redstart and Northern Wheatear can be seen. There is also a small Alpine Swift colony here. Shearwaters and Shags can be seen out at sea. Finally explore the harbour area for Audouin's Gulls. Tern species can be good here and include Black Tern, White-winged Black Tern, Whiskered Tern and Little Tern, with Sandwich Tern in the winter. There are some lovely restaurants here along the harbour front.

Arta Mountains

Arta is well signposted once you reach Alcudia. Head for Can Picafort and then onto the Arta road itself. Arta is situated on the east of the island. It is a large area with some great scenery, open spaces, pine trees and open farmland. There are plenty of paths to explore and a day could easily be spent in this area. Arta is also the site of Ses Paisses - a Bronze Age village where the whole perimeter wall is still preserved. This is also the location of a medieval fortress and underground caves.

There are several particularly well known and good birding sites within the Arta range such as Colonia Sant Pere. The road leading to this site is on the left just before you reach Arta itself. Tawny Pipit, Thekla Lark, Hoopoe, Bee Eater, Kestrel, Peregrine Falcon, Booted Eagle, Egyptian Vulture, Red Kite, Black Kite, Corn Bunting, Woodchat Shrike, Dartford Warbler, finches and buntings can all be found.

Thekla Larks are almost guaranteed at either Cala Tort or Ermita de Betlem. Check out the Depuradora (waterworks) area as well. Near to Ermita there is a small reservoir which you can still access. If you are here during the winter check this area for Red Billed Chough and Alpine Accentor. There are still many paths in Arta which I have not yet explored but I would certainly recommend spending some time here.

TWO ADDITIONAL SITES
(if staying on the east coast)

Two additional sites also on the east coast are **Mondrago National Park** and **Val Dor**. Mondrago was made a 'protected area' in 1992 and includes a diverse range of habitat such as marshes, rocky coasts, beaches, dunes, farmland, pine forest and scrub. The birding potential of this area is immense and I still have much of this area to explore and discover for myself. To date I have seen a good range of species here from harriers, wagtails, finches, buntings, larks and falcons to migrants in the spring time and water species.

Val Dor, I actually found by chance. It was during a December visit when it was raining heavily one day so I decided to take a drive rather than sit indoors. Whilst heading towards Porto Colom I noticed a right turn signposted Val Dor. The road went past a golf course and club house but at the other end the road led down to a rough track. A left turn at the end of this track took me into an open area of pines with olive and almond groves alongside. Wryneck, Firecrest and Collard Doves were present and showing well but it was the large number of Black Redstarts and Chiffchaffs that caught my attention. Thekla Larks were also showing well plus I counted three Bonelli's Warblers feeding in the pine trees a species I was not expecting to see during the winter. This is a good area for close views of Red-legged Partridges which feed in the fields.

TARGET SPECIES BIRDING

In Mallorca there are several 'must see' species. These would include Spectacled Warbler, Balearic Warbler, Moustached Warbler, Woodchat Shrike, Eleonora's Falcon, Black Vulture, Audouin's Gull and Purple Gallinule. This section of the book is specifically aimed at informing the bird watcher exactly where these birds are within an easy to find time frame and via the most direct routes to find the birds.

I know of people who have visited the island just to concentrate on finding these species as they have may only several days available to them. There are regular flights from most UK airports. Most flights tend to leave early in the morning on the outbound journey. After arrival collecting the hire car and travelling on to your hotel should take you up to around lunch time. This should allow you time after you check in to visit the Boquer Valley which would be your closest destination bird wise if based in Puerto Pollensa with perhaps a drive along the Formentor road to take in Cases Velles and the lighthouse at Cap de Formentor.

An early start around 7 or 8am on day two at the Albufera Marsh will allow you plenty of time to see the target species to be found there. The afternoon could be spent back at the Boquer Valley if you have missed any target species leaving day three to spend ample time at Cuber Reservoir in the morning followed by an afternoon visit to the Salt Pans in the south of the island. To summarise a route plan you could follow would look something like this: (refer to directions to these sites in part three):

Day one (after check in at the hotel): **Boquer Valley** - Just outside of Puerto Pollensa. Target species here include Woodchat Shrike, Blue Rock Thrush, Balearic Warbler and Wryneck. **Afternoon: Formentor road**. Take the drive up to the lighthouse stopping off at Cases Velles along the way. Target species include Eleonora's Falcon, Balearic Shearwater, Alpine Swift and Crag Martin. At Cases Velles look for Common Crossbill in the pines and migrants in the fields.

Day two: Albufera Marsh - Leave Puerto Pollensa and head towards Alcudia on the MA-2200 road. Target species are Moustached Warbler, Eleonora's Falcon, Great Reed Warbler, Cetti's Warbler, Night Heron and Purple Gallinule.

Numerous other bird species will be present.

Afternoon – S Illiot (which is close by). Return to the Boquer Valley if you still require Balearic Warbler by heading back into Puerto Pollensa in the afternoon. When returning towards Puerto Pollensa, take some time to check along the foreshore, beach and harbour area for Audouin's Gulls.

Day three: Cuber Reservoir - Take the MA-2200 road from the small roundabout by Cafe 1919 next to the Harbour in Puerto Pollensa town then along through two roundabouts onto the MA-10 road sing posted for Soller. Target species are Spectacled Warbler, Egyptian Vulture, Black Vulture, Booted Eagle, Nightingale and Firecrest.

Summary

These three sites should give you all the target species plus allowing you time to return to one of these sites if a particular target species has been missed. Use the maps in this book and the text to show you exactly where the species can be found to save you time.

At the Boquer Valley you should see Woodchat Shrike anywhere from the car park at the base and into the valley itself. But for the best chances of seeing Balearic Warbler you will need to walk at least as far as the dry stone walls which cross the valley path or even to the end of the valley just before it drops down to the sea. This will take a little time plus extra time needed to look for this species which has a tendancy to be well hidden. Black Vulture is also a possibility.

At the Albufera Marsh you will be looking for Purple Gallinule and Moustached Warbler particularly around the three canal bridges. Eleonora's Falcon are possible here as they feed over the marshes. Look in the water areas for Marbled Duck.

Cuber Reservoir will definitely give you Black Vulture and the scrub area on the left as you walk down towards the Dam is definitely the best spot for Spectacled Warbler.

Audouin's Gull can be seen along many of the coastal areas particularly along the Puerto Pollensa sea front.

If however you have been lucky and managed to see all the target species then take some time perhaps to re-visit some sites. I would recommend Cap de Formentor (MA-2210 road). Stop off at Cases Velles along the way for Common Crossbill (sub-species), Firecrest and any migrant species. Continue on to the lighthouse to look for Eleonora's Falcons which breed along the cliffs and any Balearic and Cory's Shearwaters out at sea.

The Albufereta Marsh off the MA-2200 road towards Alcudia is always worth a visit for the diverse species of water birds raptors and migrants. Eleonora's Falcons are also possible here.

There is another Balearic Warbler site at Porto Colom in the thick vegetation near to the harbour which could be visited on your return trip to the airport (depending on the flight time and keeping in mind that you need to be at the airport at least two hours before the check in time).

Above: *Woodchat Shrike. The Boquer Valley is a good site for this species.*
Below: *Purple Gallinule. The Albufera Marsh is a good site.*

All images © Cliff Woodhead unless stated

Above: *Cettis Warbler - Abundant in the marsh areas.*
Below: *Eleonora's Falcon. Cap de Formentor and The Albufera Marsh are good sites.*

Above: *Sardinian Warbler. Found anywhere where there is thick scrub*
Below: *Nesting Stone Curlew. The Boquer Valley, marsh areas and fields are good sites.*

Above: *Marsh Harrier hunting. The marshes are excellent sites*
Below: *Kentish Plover. Found in all marsh areas and at the Salt Pans*

All images © Cliff Woodhead unless stated

Above: *Purple Heron. Found anywhere in marshes and rivers.*
Below: *Crested Coot with young. The Albufera Marsh is currently the only site for this species.*

Above: *Common Terns copulating. Seen over water areas during migration*
Below: *The magnificent Bee Eater showing its nine different colours. There is a small breeding colony near to S Illiot but groups can be seen and heard when on migration.*

Above: *Great Reed Warbler. The Albufera Marsh is the best site.*
Below: *Black-winged Stilt with young. The marshes and Salt Pans are excellent sites for this species.*

Above: *Nightingale. Found anywhere and particularly where Tamarisks line the river banks.*
Below: *Collard Pratincole. The Salt Pans can be a reliable site for this species.*

Above: *Little Bittern.   The Albufera Marsh is the best site for this little heron*
Below: *Night Heron.   A common sight in the Tamarisks along the canal at the Albufera*

Above: *Curlew Sandpiper.   The Salt Pans can be an excellent site.*
Below: *Stonechat, common throughout the island.*

Above: *Audouin's Gull. Regular along the Puerto Pollensa beach and harbour.* © Neville Davies **Below:** *Cirl Bunting. The beginning of the Boquer Valley is good site for the species.*

Above: *Squacco Heron. Regular in the damp areas around the island.*
Below: *Common Crossbill. Cases Velles is an excellent site for this species, especially in or around pine trees and near roadsides.* © Neville Davies

PART FOUR

SYSTEMATIC BIRD SPECIES LIST

Species Checklist for Mallorca

To aim to keep the species list concise and less confusing I have set out the species in order as they appear in most field guides. However, the lists I have put here will differ slightly by having resident species, migrant species (including winter/autumn and spring/summer migrants), plus summer and winter visitors. Resident breeders are listed first with vagrant/accidental species listed next and finally introduced and escaped species. I believe the resident species will be of most interest to visitors then the migrants themselves.

The list itself can be used as a checklist for you to mark off each species you see. Some species may appear in several different columns as they can appear at different times of the year and in a different status such as both a migrant and winter visitor for example. There is a regional records committee known as the CRLB.

It would be very beneficial if you could take the time to forward me any sightings via my email address including where the bird was seen and at what time of the year. I will be looking at producing an annual bird report for Mallorca and sightings submitted to myself will see your name included in the report as a contributor along with where when and in what number your bird sighting occured. My email address is ecologycymru@gmail.com

Synopsis Of Species Recorded in Mallorca

This synopsis lists the species as they appear in the bird guides and uses the English name followed by the Latin name and then their status on or around the island.

Please note: Several bird names have changed in recent years as seen in many new bird guides. There are several listed in this book that would fall under this category and these include:

Original Name	New Name
Bittern	Eurasian Bittern
Purple Gallinule	Purple Swamp Hen
Avocet	Pied Avocet
Knot	Red Knot
Curlew	Eurasian Curlew
Redshank	Common Redshank
Swallow	Barn Swallow
Fan-tailed Warbler	Zitting Cisticola
Chough	Red-billed Chough
Crested Coot	Red-knobbed Coot
Sparrowhawk	Eurasian Sparrowhawk

Sightings of bird species on the island over the years have been contributed to by Graham Hearl, Mark Thompson, David Wellings, David Hanford, Ian Tillotson and of course myself and also from other bird watchers who take the time to record and send in their sightings.

Note: The Salt Pans refers to Salinas de Levante.

1. Great Crested Grebe *Podiceps cristatus*
Scarce winter visitor mainly in coastal bays in relatively small numbers.

2. Little Grebe *Tachybaptus ruficollis*
Scarce winter visitor mainly confined to coastal bays.

3. Black-necked Grebe *Podiceps nigricollis*
Winter visitor and vagrant. Can be seen offshore as well.

4. Cory's Shearwater *Calonectris diomedia*
Resident breeder on offshore islands March to August. Can be seen out at sea from the lighthouse at Cap de Formentor and from Far de Cap Sellines in the South.

5. Balearic Shearwater *Puffinus maurentanicus*
Resident breeder on offshore islands March to August. A good place to scan for this species is from the lighthouse at Cap de Formentor.

6. **Yelkouan Shearwater** *Puffinus yelokouan*
Occasional sightings offshore.

7. **Storm Petrel** *Hydrobates pelagicus*
Breeding summer visitor, occasional sightings.

8. **Gannet** *Morus bassanus*
Scarce winter visitor off the coast late October to late April.

9. **Cormorant** *Phalacrocorax carbo*
Fairly common winter visitor from September to March particularly along coastal harbours.

10. **Shag** *Phalacrocorax aristotelis*
Breeding resident. Good numbers perch on the rocks in the Puerto Pollensa bay area.

11. **Bittern** *Botaurus stellaris*
Resident and summer breeder. The Albufera Marsh can be a good site.

12. **Little Bittern** *Ixobrychus minutus*
Summer breeding visitor from March to October. Occasionally over winters especially at the Albufera Marsh.

13. **Night Heron** *Nycticorax nycticorax*
Resident breeder. The population of this species still remains relatively small. The Albufera Marsh is a stronghold.

14. **Squacco Heron** *Ardeola ralliodes*
Passage migrant in small numbers mid April to May. Occasionally over winters particularly at the S Illot and the Albufera Marsh.

15. **Cattle Egret** *Bubulcus ibis*
Winter visitor October to March, but can be seen throughout the year in small numbers anywhere where cattle are present.

16. **Great White Egret** *Egretta alba*
Winter visitor and passage migrant November to March in small numbers. The Albufereta Marsh is a good winter site.

17. **Little Egret** *Egretta garzetta*
Resident breeder and passage migrant in good numbers. Nests in the trees at the entrance of the Albufera Marsh.

18. **Grey Heron** *Ardea cinerea*
Winter visitor in small numbers. Can be seen throughout the year particularly at the Albufereta and Albufera Marshes.

19. **Purple Heron** *Ardea purpurea*
Summer visiting breeder April to September.

20. **Black Stork** *Ciconia nigra*
Rare passage migrant usually in ones and twos between April and May. The ridge above the Boquer Valley can be a good site as they pass through on migration.

21. **White Stork** *Ciconia ciconia*
Rare passage migrant mainly in ones and twos between April and May.

22. **Glossy Ibis** *Plegadis falcinellus*
Rare passage migrant April to May. Over winters in small numbers and seems to favour the Albufera Marsh. Seven sighted in the area December 2008 (ND).

23. **Spoonbill** *Platalea leucorodia*
Rare passage migrant August to October. Occasionally seen in other months of the year.

24. **Greater Flamingo** *Phoenicopterus ruber*
Migrant from early spring and winter particularly at the Salt Pans November to January. Occasionally seen flying in small numbers across Pollenca Bay early April and May during migration.

25. **Greylag Goose** *Anser anser*
Winter visitor in small numbers particularly at the Salt Pans.

26. **Common Shelduck** *Tadorna tadorna*
Scarce migrant. Winter numbers particularly at Es Trenc are increasing with over 120 there in December 2008 (ND)

27. **Wigeon** *Anas penelope*
Winter visitor October to March and occasionally into April.

28. Gadwall *Anas strepera*
Winter visitor October to April.

29. Teal *Anas crecca*
Winter visitor and passage migrant October to March. Occasionally seen during the summer months.

30. Mallard *Anas platyrhynchos*
Resident breeder.

31. Pintail *Anas acuta*
Winter visitor in small numbers September to April.

32. Garganey *Anas querquedula*
Passage migrant in small numbers February to April.

33. Shoveler *Anas clypeata*
Winter visitor generally in high numbers particuarly at the Albufera Marsh (in front of the CIM Hide is an excellent spot).

34. Red-crested Pochard *Netta rufina*
Resident. Numbers in recent years have been boosted by introduced birds.

35. Common Pochard *Aythya ferina*
Winter visitor in small numbers November to March.

36. Ferruginous Duck *Aythya nyroca*
Scarce migrant comprising of mostly single birds. Has been recorded in all months of the year. Male at the Albufereta Marsh in 2008 (ND).

37. Tufted Duck *Aythya fuligula*
Winter visitor in small numbers October to March.

38. Common Scoter *Melanitta nigra*
Scarce winter visitor. There have been several sightings off shore from Pollenca Bay in particular.

39. Red-breasted Merganser *Mergus serrator*
Very rare winter visitor.

40. White-headed Duck *Oxyura leucocephala*
Re-introduced into the Albufera Marsh. Occasional sightings but numbers still low.

41. Honey Buzzard *Pernis apivorus*
Passage migrant March to May in small numbers. Can be seen into June. Seventeen near the Mirador on the Formentor road was a good count in 2007 (ND). The ridge above the Boquer Valley can be another good spot during the early mornings during migration.

42. Common Buzzard *Buteo buteo*
Passage migrant from March to May and again August to September in small numbers.

43. Black Kite *Milvus migrans*
Passage migrant from March to May. Can be seen into September in low numbers. Albercutz Farm (near the Boquer Valley) can be a good feeding spot.

44. Red Kite *Milvus milvus*
Breeding resident and passage migrant. Cuber Reservoir is an excellent site.

45. Egyptian Vulture *Neophron percnopterus*
Resident. Possibly two to three pairs on the island. Can be seen mostly along the Tramuntana Mountain range (Soller to the Boquer Valley).

46. Black Vulture *Aegypius monachus*
Resident breeder. Numbers at Cuber Reservoir can reach up to double figures. Eighteen over Puig Major May 2007 was a particularly good count (ND).

47. Griffon Vulture *Gyps fulvus*
Resident, a single bird has been wandering the Tramuntana's range since the early 1980s. However, during December 2008 a group of 17 (ND) were circling with a single Black Vulture above Puig Major Mountain (above Cuber Reservoir). Griffon Vultures are now a regular sight in the Cuber Reservoir area and seem to have taken residence in the Tramantana Mountain range in the north of the island.

48. Booted Eagle *Hieraaetus pennatus*
Resident breeder and passage migrant. Both light phase and the more common dark phase birds occur.

49. Bonelli's Eagle *Hieraateus fasciatus*
Rare passage migrant. Single birds reported at the Boquer Valley (ND), Soller and Es Trenc (ND).

50. Marsh Harrier *Circus aeruginosus*
Resident breeder and passage migrant from March to May. Albufera and Albufereta Marshes are excellent sites.

51. Hen Harrier *Circus cyaneus*
Winter visitor in small numbers and an occasional passage migrant. Albufera Marsh can be a good wintering site for this species as can the fields off the Puerto Pollensa back roads.

52. Montagu's Harrier *Circus pygargus*
Passage migrant in very small numbers March to May. One seen at Cala San Vicente May 2009 (ND).

53. Sparrowhawk *Accipiter nisus*
Rare passage migrant and occasional winter visitor September to April.

54. Osprey *Pandion haliaetus*
Resident breeder. Marsh areas and Cuber Reservoir are good sites.

55. Kestrel *Falco tinnunculus*
Common resident breeder.

56. Red-footed Falcon *Falco vespertinus*
Rare migrant late April through to June.

57. Merlin *Falco columbarius*
Rare passage migrant April to June.

58. Hobby Falco subbuteo
Rare passage migrant April to June. Cuber Reservoir can be good for this species.

59. Peregrine Falcon *Falco peregrinus*
Resident breeder. Cap de Formentor is a good site for this species which breeds along the cliffs here

60. **Eleonora's Falcon** *Falco eleonorae*
Summer visiting breeder arrival late April and staying until October. Regularly hunts over themarsh areas, and can sometimes be seen drinking at the edge of the reservoir at Cuber.

61. **Little Owl** *Athene noctua*
I have seen this species however on the mountain roads at any time of the year, particularly during evening drives where I have watched them eating beetles on the road.

62. **Tawny Owl** *Strix aluco*
Found throughout the island in small numbers.

63. **Red-legged Partridge** *Alectoris rufa*
Resident breeder in good numbers.

64. **Quail** *Coturnix coturnix*
Passage migrant and breeder. The crop fields at Albufereta Marsh can be a good site.

65. **Pheasant** *Phasianus colchicus*
Resident breeder which is now quite well established considering it has been introduced.

66. **Water Rail** *Rallus aquaticus*
Resident breeder. The Salt Pans is an excellent site for this species.

67. **Spotted Crake** *Porzana poprzana*
Migrant summer breeder arriving in March. Not an easy bird to find and records are not that common.

68. **Moorhen** *Gallinula chloropus*
Common resident breeder.

69. **Purple Gallinule** *Porphyrio porphyrio*
Breeding resident in all wetland areas except the Salt Pans. This species was re-introduced as part of a breeding program in 1991, and their status continues to improve. Numerous pairs can be found at both the Albufera and Albufereta Marshes and S Illot (Depuodora site).

70. **Coot** *Fulica atra*
Common resident breeder.

71. **Common Crane** *Grus grus*
Scarce passage migrant April to May.

72. **Oystercatcher** *Haematopus ostralegus*
Rare passage migrant April to May and from August to October.

73. **Black-winged Stilt** *Himantopos himantopos*
Resident breeder in good numbers.

74. **Avocet** *Recurvirostra avosetta*
Migrant in small numbers.   Has been seen in every month of the year.   The Salt Pans is an excellent site.

75. **Collard Pratincole** *Glareola pratincola*
Migrant April to May.   The Salt Pans is a good location on the open mud area just past the three palm trees.

76. **Little Ringed Plover** *Charadrius dubius*
Breeding summer visitor from March until October.

77. **Ringed Plover** *Charadrius hiaticula*
Passage migrant from March to May and again from September to October. There are occasional winter sightings especially at the Salt Pans.

78. **Kentish Plover** *Charadrius alexandrius*
Common resident breeder.

79. **Golden Plover** *Pluvialis apricara*
Scarce passage migrant and occasional winter visitor.

80. **Grey Plover** *Pluvialis squatarola*
Scare passage migrant from March to May and again September to October. Occasional winter sightings at the Salt Pans in small numbers.

81. **Lapwing** *Vanellus vanellus*
Winter visitor from October through to March.   S Illot is a particularly good site.

82. **Knot** *Calidris canutus*
Scarce passage migrant May to September.

83. **Sanderling** *Calidris alba*
Scarce passage migrant from April to May in small numbers.

84. **Little Stint** *Calidris minuta*
Common passage migrant March to April and again September to October. Winter sightings are likely particularly at the Salt Pans.

85. **Temminck's Stint** *Calidris temminckii*
Scarce passage migrant from September through to April. Occasional winter records. Check carefully through Little Stint flocks as the two species regularly feed together.

86. **Curlew Sandpiper** *Calidris furruginea*
Passage migrant from April to May and again September to October.

87. **Dunlin** *Calidris alpina*
Passage migrant from March to April and again September to October. Also a winter visitor particularly at the Salt Pans.

88. **Ruff** *Philomachus pugnax*
Common passage migrant March to April and again September to October. Small numbers occasionally over winter.

89. **Common Snipe** *Gallinage gallinago*
Common winter visitor from September through to early May.

90. **Jack Snipe** *Lymnocryptes minimus*
Scarce winter visitor October through to March.

91. **Woodcock** *Scolopax rusticola*
Rare winter visitor October through to March.

92. **Bar-tailed Godwit** *Limosa lapponica*
Scarce passage migrant May to September with occasional winter sightings. Small numbers occur at the Salt Pans.

93. **Black-tailed Godwit** *Limosa limosa*
Passage migrant from March to April and again September to October.
Occasional winter sightings in small numbers.

94. **Curlew** *Numenius arquata*
Winter visitor and passage migrant September through to March.

95. **Whimbrel** *Numenius phaeopus*
Passage migrant in small numbers in April and during the autumn months.

96. **Stone Curlew** *Burhinus oedicnemeus*
Resident breeder. The stone fields in the Boquer Valley are a good site.

97. **Spotted Redshank** *Tringa erythropus*
Passage migrant from March to May.   Occasional winter sightings.

98. **Common Redshank** *Tringa totanus*
Passage migrant March to May, also September to October and occasional winter
sightings occur.

99. **Marsh Sandpiper** *Tringa stagnatilis*
Passage migrant in very small numbers from April to May and September to
October. Albufera Marsh from the Bishop 1 Hide can be a good place to see them.

100. **Greenshank** *Tringa nebularia*
Passage migrant April to May and September to October.

101. **Common Sandpiper** *Actitis hypoleucos*
Passage migrant from March to April and September to October with winter
sightings fairly common.

102. **Green Sandpiper** *Tringa ochropus*
Passage migrant and winter visitor. Can be seen during any month of the year in
small numbers.

103. **Wood Sandpiper** *Tringa glareola*
Common passage migrant March to May and September to October.   The
Albufera Marsh is the best site to see this species.

104. **Great Skua** *Catharacta skua*
Rare winter visitor.

105. **Mediterranean Gull** *Larus melanocephalus*
Scarce migrant occasionally seen from August to September.

106. **Little Gull** *Larus minutus*
Rare passage migrant March to May.

107. **Black-headed Gull** *Larus ridibundus*
Common passage migrant from August through to March.

108. **Slender-billed Gull** *Larus genei*
Rare migrant from April to June and August to September in low numbers.

109. **Audouin's Gull** *Larus audouinii*
Resident breeder with numbers steadily increasing. Puerto Pollensa beach is an excellent site. They tend to winter in the south of the island with only a few pairs remaining in the north.

110. **Yellow-legged Gull** *Larus cachinnans*
Common resident breeder.

111. **Lesser-black Backed Gull** *Larus fuscus*
Scarce passage migrant from August to early December.

112. **Common Tern** *Sterna hirundo*
Very rare migrant with sightings involving mostly single birds.

113. **Sandwich Tern** *Sterna sandviciensis*
Winter visitor and passage migrant.   Harbours and exposed rocks off-shore can be particularly good areas for this species.

114. **Caspian Tern** *Sterna caspia*
Very rare passage migrant during April and occasionally in June, mostly single numbers.

115. **Gull-billed Tern** *Gelochelidon nilotica*
Passage migrant from April to May and again September to October in small numbers.

116. **Little Tern** *Sterna albifrons*
Scarce passage migrant mainly from April to May.

117. **Whiskered Tern** *Childonias hybridus*
Passage migrant from March to May and occasionally September to October.

118. **Black Tern** *Childonias niger*
Passage migrant from April to May with lower numbers during the autumn months.

119. **White-winged Black Tern** *Childonias leucopterus*
Passage migrant from April to May again with smaller numbers during the autumn months.

120. **Razorbill** *Alca torda*
Scarce winter visitor off shore mostly during December and January.

121. **Puffin** *Fratercula arctica*
Scare winter visitor off shore rom January through to March.

122. **Woodpigeon** *Columba palumbus*
Resident breeder.

123. **Collard Dove** *Streptopelia decaocto*
Resident breeder.

124. **Turtle Dove** *Streptopelia turtur*
Passage migrant and summer breeder in low numbers from April to May and September to October.   Olive groves can be particularly good areas for this species.

125. **Rock Dove** *Columba livia*
Resident breeder. Those in the mountain areas such as the Boquer, Arta and along sections of the coast are pure wild birds.

126. **Cuckoo** *Cuculus canorus*
Passage migrant which arrives in April. A few pairs stay on to breed. Cuber Reservoir is a good site.

127. **Scops Owl** *Otus Scops*
Resident breeder. Can be found roosting by day especially in Pines and Eucalyptus trees.

128. **Barn Owl** *Tyto alba*
Resident breeder.

129. **Long Eared Owl** *Asio otus*
Resident breeder.

130. **Short Eared Owl** *Asio flammeus*
Rare passage migrant September through to March.

131. **Nightjar** *Caprimulgus europeus*
Passage migrant from April to May and again September to October. Can occasionally be seen on the road side especially during an evening drive in the mountains especially along the Formentor road and the Cuber roads.

132. **Common Swift** *Apus apus*
Passage migrant from April to May and again September to October. Breeds all over the island and can be seen in large numbers when feeding over the Albufera Marsh.

133. **Pallid Swift** *Apus pallidus*
Breeding summer visitor arriving in April. There are small breeding populations around some coastal locations such as the Mirador on the Formentor Road.

134. **Alpine Swift** *Apus melba*
Breeding summer visitor arriving in April. Castell de Santuri has a small breeding population of a few pairs. Check amongst flocks of Common Swifts for the odd Alpine Swift mixed in.

135. **Kingfisher** *Alcedo atthis*
Winter visitor from September through to March.

136. **Bee Eater** *Merops apiaster*
Common passage migrant April to May and July to September. Can occur on passage in large numbers. There are occasional summer breeding records particularly in the sand banks in the S Illot area (near to the Albufera reserve).

137. **Roller** *Coracias garrulus*
Rare passage migrant in very small numbers from April to late May. Cases Velles can be a good site on the telephone wires over the fields. Similarly the

Puerto Pollensa back roads can also be good sites for this species again, usually on the telephone wires.

138. **Hoopoe** *Upupa epops*
Common resident breeder.

139. **Wryneck** *Jynx torquilla*
This is the only species of woodpecker to occur on the island. A breeding resident favouring olive groves and cork oak woodlands. Also a passage migrant from March to April.

140. **Thekla Lark** *Galerida theklae*
Common resident breeder. Arta is a good location for this species as is the Albufereta Marsh.

141. **Skylark** *Alauda arvensis*
Winter visitor in high numbers from October through to March.

142. **Short-toed Lark** *Calandrella brachydactyla*
Passage migrant from April to September and also a breeding summer visitor.

143. **Crag Martin** *Hirundo rupestris*
Common resident breeder. This species spends a lot of time feeding over marshes during the winter as well as in the mountains.

144. **Sand Martin** *Riparia riparia*
Passage migrant from March to May and August to October.

145. **Swallow** *Hirudo rustica*
Common passage migrant March to May and September to October. Also a breeding summer visitor.

146. **Red-rumped Swallow** *Hirundo daurica*
Passage migrant March to May with lower numbers September to October. Check amongst hirundine flocks for this species which can mix in.

147. **House Martin** *Delichon urbica*
Passage migrant from March to May and also a summer breeder.

148. **Richard's Pipit** *Anthus novaeseelandiae*
Very scarce winter visitor, October through to April.

149. **Tawny Pipit** *Anthus campestris*
Breeding summer visitor from April through to September. Cuber Reservoir is an excellent site.

150. **Tree Pipit** *Anthus trivialis*
Passage migrant from April to May and again September to October.

151. **Meadow Pipit** *Anthus pratensis*
Common winter visitor from October through to March.

152. **Red-throated Pipit** *Anthus cervinus*
Scarce passage migrant from April to May and occasionally September to October.

153. **Water Pipit** *Anthus spinoletta*
Winter visitor from October through to March.

154. **Yellow Wagtail** *Motacilla flava (sub-species iberiae)*
Passage migrant from March to May, and again September to October. A common summer breeder.

155. **Grey Wagtail** *Motacilla cinerea*
Winter visitor from September through to March.

156. **White Wagtail** *Motacilla alba*
Common winter visitor from October through to March.

157. **Wren** *Troglodytes troglodytes*
Common breeding resident.

158. **Dunnock** *Prunella modularis*
Winter visitor in small numbers from October through to April.

159. **Alpine Accentor** *Prunella collaris*
Regular winter visitor in low numbers from November through to March. It is worth checking in any of the mountain areas. Arta is a good site for this species.

160. **Robin** *Erithacus rubecula*
Very common winter visitor from October through to March.

161. **Rufous Bush Robin** *Cercottrichas galactotes*
Very scarce spring migrant in very low numbers.

162. **Nightingale** *Luscinia megarhynchos*
Common breeding summer visitor from April through to October.

163. **Bluethroat** *Luscinia svecica*
Winter visitor from October through to March. Usually confined to wet scrub areas such as the Salt Pans.

164. **Common Redstart** *Phoenicurus phoenicurus*
Common passage migrant April to May and again September to October.

165. **Black Redstart** *Phoenicurus ochruros*
Very common winter visitor from October through to early April. Found all over the island.

166. **Stonechat** *Saxicola torquata*
Common resident breeder.

167. **Whinchat** *Saxicola ruberta*
Passage migrant from April to May and September to October.   Cases Velles can be a good site.

168. **Northern Wheatear** *Oenanthe oenanthe*
Passage migrant from March to May and September to October.

169. **Black-eared Wheatear** *Oenanthe hispanica*
Passage migrant in low numbers March to May.

170. **Blue Rock Thrush** *Monticola solitarius*
Common resident breeder.

171. **Rock Thrush** *Monticola saxatilis*
Passage migrant from April to May.   Breeds in low numbers.   Cuber Reservoir (just past the dam) is one such site though they can take some finding.

172. **Blackbird** *Turdus merula*
Common resident breeder.

173. **Ring Ouzel** *Turdus torquatus*
Scarce passage migrant March to April and September to October with occasional winter sightings.

174. **Song Thrush** *Turdus philomelos*
Common winter visitor.

175. **Mistle Thrush** *Turdus viscivorous*
Winter visitor in small numbers.

176. **Redwing** *Turdus iliaus*
Scarce winter visitor October through to March.

177. **Fieldfare** *Turdus pilaris*
Scarce winter visitor usually in low numbers.

178. **Cetti's Warbler** *Cettia cetti*
Very common resident breeder. Extremely vocal in marshy areas.

179. **Fan-tailed Warbler** *Cisticola juncidis*
Very common resident breeder.

180. **Grasshopper Warbler** *Locustella naevia*
Rare passage migrant late April to May with very low numbers September to October.

181. **Moustached Warbler** *Acrocephalus melanopogon*
Resident breeder especially at the Albufera Marsh where the population is well over three and a half thousand pairs and steadily rising.

182. **Sedge Warbler** *Acrocephalus schoenobaenus*
Very scarce passage migrant March to May and September to October.

183. **Reed Warbler** *Acrocephalus scirpaceus*
Breeding summer visitor.

184. **Great Reed Warbler** *Acrocephalus arundinaceus*
Summer breeder April through to October.

185. **Olivaceous Warbler** *Hippolais pallida*
Very scarce passage migrant late September to October.

186. **Icterine Warbler** *Hippolais icterina*
Very scarce passage migrant April to May and occasionally September to October.

187. **Melodious Warbler** *Hippolais polyglotta*
Very scarce passage migrant late April to May and occasionally September to October.

188. **Balearic Warbler** *Sylvia balearica (sub-species balearica)*
Breeding resident in garigue vegetation in both coastal and mountain areas.

189. **Dartford Warbler** *Sylvia undata*
Scarce winter visitor November through to March and an occasional very rare breeder.

190. **Spectacled Warbler** *Sylvia conspicillata*
Summer breeding visitor in small numbers. Cuber Reservoir is a good location.

191. **Subalpine Warbler** *Sylvia cantillans (sub-species moltonii)*
Passage migrant March to May and summer breeder in low numbers.

192. **Common Whitethroat** *Sylvia communis*
Passage migrant April to May and September to October.

193. **Garden Warbler** *Sylvia borin*
Passage migrant in fairly low numbers from April to May and September to October.

194. **Blackcap** *Sylvia atricapilla*
Common resident breeder. Also an occasional winter visitor.

195. **Bonelli's Warbler** *Phylloscopus bonelli*
Passage migrant in fairly low numbers April to May.

196. **Wood Warbler** *Phylloscopus sibilatrix*
Passage migrant April to May.

197. **Willow Warbler** *Phylloscopus trochilus*
Common passage migrant March to May.

198. Chiffchaff *Phylloscopus collybita*
Passage migrant March to May and a winter visitor in high numbers.

199. Goldcrest *Regulus regulus*
Winter visitor in low numbers, September through to March.

200. Firecrest *Regulus ignicapillus*
Common resident breeder.

201. Spotted Flycatcher *Musicapa striata (sub-species balearica)*
Passage migrant April to May and summer breeder in high numbers.

202. Pied Flycatcher *Ficedula hypoleuca*
Common passage migrant April to May and again September to October.

203. Great Tit *Parus major*
Common resident breeder.

204. Blue Tit *Parus caeruleus*
Common resident breeder.

205. Penduline Tit *Remiz pendulinus*
Very scarce winter visitor.

206. Golden Oriole *Oriolus oriolus*
Passage migrant April to June.

207. Woodchat Shrike *Lanius senator*
Common breeding summer visitor. Cork Oak and Olive groves can be excellent areas.

208. Red-backed Shrike *Lanius collurio*
Very scarce migrant during May and again September to October. Cases Velles is worth checking for this species on migration.

209. Raven *Corvus corax*
Common resident breeder.

210. Chough *Pyrrhocorax pyrrhocorax*
Very scarce winter visitor. The Arta Mountains are probably the only site where

one has a reasonable chance of seeing them albeit in very low numbers.

211. Common Starling *Sturnus vulgaris*
Extremely common winter visitor from October through to March. The Albufera Marsh is an excellent spot at the S Illot viewing platform to watch over one and a half million birds coming into roost.

212. House Sparrow *Passer domesticus*
Common breeding resident.

213. Tree Sparrow *Passer montanus*
Scarce resident with small populations. Single birds can occasionally be seen. However, there is a small population of up to ten birds at the Albufereta Marsh just before the water ditch.

214. Rock Sparrow *Petronia petronia*
Rare resident in much localised locations.

215. Chaffinch *Fringilla coelebs*
Common resident breeder.

216. Brambling *Fringilla montifringilla*
Winter visitor in very low numbers, October through to March. Numbers can increase during very cold weather.

217. Greenfinch *Carduelis chloris*
Very common resident breeder.

218. Goldfinch *Carduelis carduelis*
Very common resident breeder.

219. Siskin *Carduelis spinus*
Winter visitor from October through to March.

220. Linnet *Carduelis cannabina*
Very common resident breeder.

221. Serin *Serinus serinus*
Very common resident breeder.

222. Common Crossbill *Loxia curvirostra (sub-species balearica)*
Very common resident breeder found anywhere where there are pine trees present.

223. Hawfinch *Coccothraustes coccothraustes*
Scarce migrant March to May and scarce winter visitor October through to March.

224. Corn Bunting *Miliaria calandra*
Very common resident breeder in farmland areas.

225. Cirl Bunting *Emberiza cirlus*
Very common resident breeder.

226. Reed Bunting *Emberiza schoeniculua*
Resident breeder and winter visitor October through to April.

Vagrants and Accidentals

The term vagrant or accidental refers to a species which would not normally be expected to turn up in any particular area. Basically this means that a bird has arrived by accident such as being blown off course during strong winds. Other factors can occur such as when birds are on reverse migration and overshooting their migration routes.

I am continuing the list of species recorded in Mallorca by keeping vagrants and accidentals as a separate but continual list following species 1 to 226. The following species have been recorded in various parts of the island and off shore. The year and location has been included.

The sightings however are not exhaustive and many of these species have been recorded more than once.

227. Red-necked Grebe *Podiceps grisegena*
Albufera Marsh 1985 and 1987.

228. Slavonian Grebe *Podiceps auritus*
The Salt Pans in 1985.

229. **African Spoonbill** *Platalea alba*
One at the Albufera Marsh 1988.

230. **Lesser Flamingo** *Phoenicopterus minor*
One at the Salt Pans 1988.

231. **Mute Swan** *Cygnus olor*
Seen at the Albufera Marsh but possibly consist of escaped birds.

232. **Bean Goose** *Anser fabalis*
One at the Salt Pans 2008 (ND).

233. **White-fronted Goose** *Anser albifrons*
The Albufera Marsh 1992 and 1996.

234. **Egyptian Goose** *Alopochen aegyptiacus*
Possible feral flock sighted which could be from France where a small group had
been previously recorded.

235. **Ruddy Shelduck** *Tadorna ferruginea*
Seen at the Albufera Marsh 1988 and at the Salt Pans 1998.

236. **Mandarin Duck** *Aix galericulata*
One at the Albufera Marsh 1990.

237. **Blue-winged Teal** *Anas discors*
One at the Albufera Marsh 1997.

238. **Marbled Teal** *Marmaronetta angusterostris*
The Salt Pans.   The actual year this species was recorded is uncertain.

239. **Eider** *Somateria mollissima*
One seen in Palma Bay 1987.

240. **Long Tailed Duck** *Clangula hyemalis*
Two at the Salt Pans 1994.

241. **Goldeneye** *Bucephala clangula*
Depuodora (S Illot) 1998 in small numbers.

242. Goosander *Mergus merganser*
Small group seen in Palma during 1990.

243. Short-toed Eagle *Circaetus gallicus*
One at the Formentor Peninsula 1994.

244. Pallid Harrier *Circus macrourus*
One at Cases Velles 1994.

245. Lesser Kestrel *Falco naumanni*
The location is uncertain of where this species has been seen however there are two records from 1985 and 1997.

246. Lanner Falcon *Falco biarmicus*
One at the Albufera Marsh 1990.

247. Little Crake *Porzana parva*
Occasionally seen at the Albufera Marsh during spring.

248. Baillon's Crake *Porzana pusilla*
One at the Albufera Marsh (year uncertain).

249. Corncrake *Crex crex*
One at the Albufera Marsh (year uncertain).

250. Cream Coloured Courser *Cursorius cursor*
One at the Albufera Marsh 1988.

251. Black-winged Pratincole *Glareola nordmanni*
One at the Se Illiot site during 1991.

252. Dotterel *Charadrius morinellus*
Single birds seen during 1985 1991 and 1997 at Depuradora (the waterworks site near to the Albufera Marsh) and Cap de Sallines (near the Salt Pans area).

253. Pectoral Sandpiper *Calidris melanotos*
One at Salobrar de Campos 1988.

254. Buff-breasted Sandpiper *Tryngites subruficollis*
One at Pollenca Bay 1994. This record was accepted.

255. Great Snipe *Gallinago media*
Single records from the Albufera Marsh during 1989, 1990, 1991 and 1995.

256. Slender-billed Curlew *Numenius tenuirostris*
One at the Albufera Marsh 1988.

257. Greater Yellowlegs *Tringa nebularia*
One at Salobrar de Campos 1995.

258. Terek Sandpiper *Xenus cinereus*
One at the Albufera Marsh in 1992 and Salobrar de Campos 1994.

259. Red-necked Phalarope *Phalaropus lobatus*
One at the Albufera Marsh 1989.

260. Arctic Skua *Stercorarius parasiticus*
One over the Albufera Marsh 1988 and one at Porto Colom 1992.

261. Long-tailed Skua *Stercorarius longicaudus*
One at the Salines de S Illot 1991.

262. Common Gull *Larus canus*
Various sightings in 1985.

263. Herring Gull *Larus argentatus*
Two at S Illot 1997.

264. Kittiwake *Rissa tridactyla*
Cap de Pinar 1991. There are occasional off shore sightings of this species from around the island particularly from the south.

265. Lesser Crested Tern *Sterna bengalensis*
One at the S Illot 1997.

266. Roseate Tern *Sterna dougallii*
Two at the Albufera Marsh 1991.

267. Great Spotted Cuckoo *Clamator glandarius*
One seen at Felanitx in 1988 and one at the Boquer Valley in 1991.

268. **Yellow-billed Cuckoo** *Coccyzus americanus.*
A first year bird was found dead at Cala Millor (east coast) in 1994.

269. **Bar-tailed Desert Lark** *Ammomanes cinturus*
One at Cap de Ses Salines 1994.

270. **White-winged Lark** *Melanocorypha leucoptera*
One recorded at Montuiri 1986.

271. **Lesser Short-toed Lark** *Calandrella rufescens*
Recorded at the Albufera Marsh between 1988 and 1993.

272. **Woodlark** *Lullula arborea*
One at Port de Pollensa 1995.

273. **Olive-backed Pipit** *Anthus hodgsoni*
One at Cases Velles 1990.

274. **Rock Pipit** *Anthus petrosus*
Albufera Marsh 1993 and S Illot in the same year. This was probably the same bird moving around.

275. **Citrine Wagtail** *Motacilla citreola*
Single birds recorded at the Albufera Marsh 1987 and S Illot 1997.

276. **Savi's Warbler** *Locustella luscinioides*
Sighted 1985 – 1992 from several locations.

277. **Aquatic Warbler** *Acrocephalus paludicola*
Sighted 1989 – 1997 from several locations.

278. **Marsh Warbler** *Acrocephalus palustris*
One at the Formentor Lighthouse 1994.

279. **Orphean Warbler** *Sylvia hortensis*
One at the Boquer Valley 1996.

280. **Pallas's Warbler** *Phylloscopus proregulua*
One recorded at Mortitx 1995.

281. Yellow-browed Warbler *Phylloscopus inoratus*
Recorded in the Boquer Valley in 1989 and 1996 and at Cases Velles 1992 and 1996.

282. Red-breasted Flycatcher *Ficedula parva*
One at the Albufera Marsh 1987.

283. Semi-collard Flycatcher *Ficedula semitorquata*
Sighted by myself at the base of the Boquer Valley 1992.

284. Collard Flycatcher *Ficedula albicollis*
Cases Velles 1990, Salobrar de Campos 1993 and the Boquer Valley 1997.

285. Coal Tit *Parus ater*
One feeding in vegetation around the Torrente de Pareis 1995.

286. Wallcreeper *Tichodroma muraria*
One sighted on the face of the ridge at Ternelles Valley 1985.

287. Great Grey Shrike *Lanius excubitor*
Seen at the Arta Mountains in 1992 and Salobrar de Campos in 1994.

288. Masked Shrike *Lanius nubicus*
Single birds recorded at Cases Velles and the Boquer valley in 1991.

289. Spotless Starling *Sturnus unicolor*
Seen during 1994 from several locations in the north of the island.

290. Snow Finch *Montifringilla nivalis*
One seen at Puig Major (highest mountain above Cuber Reservoir) in 1985 and 1986, Albercutz Valley (down from the Boquer Valley) in 1993 and Tomir in 1996.

291. Citril Finch *Serinus citrinella*
One at Cases Velles 1994.

292. Trumpeter Finch *Bucanetes githagineus*
One at Porto Colom in 1994, Cap de Sellines in 1997 and Albufera Marsh 1998 (the latter record seen by myself).

293. Snow Bunting *Plectrophenax nivalis*
One at the Depuradora (S Illot) 1998.

294. Yellowhammer *Emberiza citrinella*
Cala Sant Vicente 1987.

295. Rock Bunting *Emberiza cia*
Mortitx 1985, Cuber 1987, Albufera 1990 and base of the Boquer Valley 1997 (latter record seen by myself).

296. Little Bunting *Emberiza pusilla*
One at Cases Velles in 1991 and Mortitx 1991.

There are several other species recorded as vagrants on the neighbouring small islands which belong to the Balearics such as Cabrera and Dragonera. These would include: Swinhoe's Petrel, Marsh Warbler, Orphean Warbler, Lesser Whitethroat, Radde's Warbler, Scarlet Rosefinch, Bullfinch and Yellow-breasted Bunting (all accepted records).

The following species lists are set out as a tick list to remind you what species you seen during your trip.

Resident Species			
English Name	**Latin/Scientific Name**	**Year Seen**	**Tick**
Little Grebe	*Tachybaptus ruficollis*		
Cory's Shearwater	*Calonectris diomedea*		
Balearic Shearwater	*Puffinus mauretanicus*		
Shag	*Phalacrocorax aristoelis*		
Night Heron	*Nycticorax nycticorax*		
Cattle Egret	*Bubulcus ibis*		
Little Egret	*Egretta garzetta*		
Grey Heron	*Ardea cinera*		
Mallard	*Anas platyrhynchos*		
Red Crested Pochard	*Netta rufina*		

Resident Species (cont'd)

English Name	Latin/Scientific Name	Year Seen	Tick
Red Kite	Milvus milvus		
Egyptian Vulture	Neophron percnopterus		
Black Vulture	Aegypius monachus		
Marsh Harrier	Circus aeruginosus		
Booted Eagle	Hieraetus pennatus		
Osprey	Pandion haliaetus		
Kestrel	Falco tinnunculus		
Peregrine Falcon	Falco peregrinus		
Red-legged Partridge	Alectoris rufa		
Water Rail	Rallus aquaticus		
Moorhen	Gallinula chloropus		
Coot	Fulica atra		
Black Winged Stilt	Himantopus himantopus		
Stone Curlew	Burhinus oedicnemus		
Little Ringed Plover	Charadrius dubius		
Kentish Plover	Charadrius alexandrinus		
Common Redshank	Tringa totanus		
Audouin's Gull	Larus audouinii		
Yellow-legged Gull	Larus cachinnans		
Rock Dove	Columba livia		
Woodpigeon	Columba palumbus		
Collard Dove	Streptopelia decaocto		
Barn Owl	Tyto alba		
Scops Owl	Otus scops		
Long-eared Owl	Asio otus		
Hoopoe	Upupa epops		
Wryneck	Jynx torquilla		
Thekla Lark	Galerida theklae		
Crag Martin	Hirundo rupestris		
Wrent	Troglodytes troglodytes		

Resident Species (cont'd)			
English Name	**Latin/Scientific Name**	**Year Seen**	**Tick**
Stonechat	*Saxicola torquata*		
Blue Rock Thrush	*Monticola solitarus*		
Blackbird	*Turdus merula*		
Cetti's Warbler	*Cettia cetti*		
Fan-tailed Warbler	*Cisticola juncidis*		
Moustached Warbler	*Acrocephalus melanopogon*		
Balearic Warbler	*Sylvia balearica*		
Dartford Warbler	*Sylvia undata*		
Sardinian Warbler	*Sylvia melanocephala*		
Blackcap	*Sylvia atricapilla*		
Firecrest	*Regulus ignicapillus*		
Blue Tit	*Parus caeruleus*		
Great Tit	*Parus major*		
Raven	*Corvus corax*		
House Sparrow	*Passer domesticus*		
Tree Sparrow	*Passer montanus*		
Chaffinch	*Fringilla coelebs*		
Serin	*Serinus serinus*		
Greenfinch	*Carduelis chloris*		
Goldfinch	*Carduelis carduelis*		
Linnet	*Carduelis cannabina*		
Crossbill	*Loxia curvirostra*		
Cirl Bunting	*Emberiza cirlus*		
Reed Bunting	*Emberiza schoeniclus*		
Corn Bunting	*Miliaria calandra*		

Migrants (Autumn/Winter & Spring/Summer)			
English Name	**Latin/Scientific Name**	**Year Seen**	**Tick**
Black-necked Grebe	*Podiceps nigricollis*		
Spotted Crake	*Porzana porzana*		
Avocet	*Recurvirostra avosetta*		
Ringed Plover	*Charadrius hiaticula*		
Grey Plover	*Pluvialis squatarola*		
Curlew Sandpiper	*Calidris ferruginea*		
Dunlin	*Calidris alpina*		
Ruff	*Philomachus pugnax*		
Black-tailed Godwit	*Limosa limosa*		
Whimbrel	*Numenius phaeops*		
Spotted Redshank	*Tringa erythropus*		
Marsh Sandpiper	*Tringa stagnatilis*		
Green Sandpiper	*Tringa ochropus*		
Common Sandpiper	*Actitis hypoleucos*		
Gull-billed Tern	*Gelochelidon nilotica*		
Little Tern	*Sterna albifrons*		
Whiskered Tern	*Chidonias hybridus*		
Black tern	*Chidonias niger*		
White-winged Black Tern	*Chidonias leucopterus*		
Nightjar	*Caprimulgus europaeus*		
Sand Martin	*Riparia riparia*		
Red-rumped Swallow	*Hirundo daurica*		
Tree Pipit	*Anthus trivialis*		
Common Redstart	*Phoenicurus phoenicurus*		
Whinchat	*Saxicola ruberta*		
Northern Wheatear	*Oenanthe oenanthe*		
Black-eared Wheatear	*Oenanthe hispanica*		
Icterine Warbler	*Hippolais icterina*		
Melodious Warbler	*Hippolais polyglotta*		
Subalpine Warbler	*Sylvia cantillans*		

Migrants - Autumn/Winter & Spring/Summer (cont'd)

English Name	Latin/Scientific Name	Year Seen	Tick
Whitethroat	*Sylvia communis*		
Garden warbler	*Sylvia borin*		
Bonelli's Warbler	*Phylloscopus bonelli*		
Wood Warbler	*Phylloscopus sibilatrix*		
Willow Warbler	*Philloscopus trochilus*		
Pied Flycatcher	*Ficedula hypoleuca*		
Ortolan Bunting	*Emberiza hortulana*		

Rare Migrants

English Name	Latin/Scientific Name	Year Seen	Tick
Yelkouan Shearwater	*Puffinus yelkouan*		
Gannet	*Morus bassanus*		
Black Stork	*Ciconia nigra*		
White Stork	*Ciconia ciconia*		
Glossy Ibis	*Pleagadis falcinellus*		
Spoonbill	*Platalea leucorodia*		
Greater Flamingo	*Phoenicopterus ruber*		
Shelduck	*Tadorna tadorna*		
Ferruginous Duck	*Aythya nyroca*		
Griffon Vulture	*Gyps fulvus*		
Sparrowhawk	*Accipiter nisus*		
Merlin	*Falco columbaris*		
Hobby	*Falco subbuteo*		
Common Crane	*Grus grus*		
Oystercatcher	*Haematopus ostralegus*		
Knot	*Calidris cantus*		
Sanderling	*Calidris alba*		
Temminck's Stint	*Calidris temminckii*		
Bar-tailed Godwit	*Limosa lapponica*		
Turnstone	*Arenaria interpres*		

Rare Migrants (cont'd)			
English Name	**Latin/Scientific Name**	**Year Seen**	**Tick**
Mediterranean Gull	*Larus melanocephalus*		
Little Gull	*Larus minitus*		
Slender-billed Gull	*Larus genei*		
Lesser Black-backed Gull	*Larus fuscus*		
Short-eared Owl	*Asio flammeus*		
Roller	*Coracias garrulus*		
Red-throated Pipit	*Anthus cervinus*		
Grasshopper Warbler	*Locustella naevia*		
Sedge Warbler	*Acrocephalus schoenobaenus*		
Olivaceous Warbler	*Hippolais pallida*		
Red-backed Shrike	*Lanius collurio*		
Tree Sparrow	*Passer montanus*		
Brambling	*Fringilla montifringilla*		

Summer Visitors			
English Name	**Latin/Scientific Name**	**Year Seen**	**Tick**
Storm petrel	*Hydrobates pelagicus*		
Bittern	*Botaurus stellaris*		
Little Bittern	*Ixobrychus minutus*		
Purple Heron	*Ardea purpurea*		
Eleonora's Falcon	*Falco eleonorae*		
Quail	*Coturnix coturnix*		
Little Ringed Plover	*Charadrius dubius*		
Turtle Dove	*Streptopelia turtur*		
Cuckoo	*Cuculus canorus*		
Alpine Swift	*Apus melba*		
Common Swift	*Apus apus*		
Pallid Swift	*Apus pallidus*		
Bee-eater	*Merops apiaster*		
Short-toed Lark	*Calandrella brachdactya*		

Summer Visitors (cont'd)

English Name	Latin/Scientific Name	Year Seen	Tick
Swallow	*Hirundo rustica*		
House Martin	*Delichon urbica*		
Tawny Pipit	*Anthus campestris*		
Yellow Wagtail	*Motacilla flava*		
Nightingale	*Luscinia megarhynchos*		
Rock Thrush	*Monticola saxatillis*		
Reed Warbler	*Acrocephalus scirpaceus*		
Great Reed Warbler	*Acrocephalus arundinaceus*		
Spectacled Warbler	*Sylvia conspicillata*		
Subalpine Warbler	*Sylvia cantillans*		
Spotted Flycatcher	*Musciapa striata*		
Balearic Woodchat Shrike	*Lanius senator baddius*		

Winter Visitors

English Name	Latin/Scientific Name	Year Seen	Tick
Great Crested Grebe	*Podiceps cristatus*		
Black-necked Grebe	*Podiceps nigricollis*		
Cormorant	*Phalacrocorax carbo*		
Cattle Egret	*Bubulcus ibis*		
Great White Egret	*Egretta alba*		
Greylag Goose	*Anser anser*		
Wigeon	*Anas penelope*		
Gadwall	*Anas strepera*		
Teal	*Anas crecca*		
Pintail	*Anas acuta*		
Shoveler	*Anas clypeata*		
Pochard	*Aythya ferina*		
Tufted Duck	*Aythya fuligula*		
Hen Harrier	*Circus cyaneus*		
Common Buzzard	*Buteo buteo*		

Winter Visitors (cont'd)			
English Name	**Latin/Scientific Name**	**Year Seen**	**Tick**
Golden Plover	*Pluvialis apricaria*		
Grey Plover	*Pluvialis squatarola*		
Lapwing	*Vanellus vanellus*		
Little Stint	*Calidris minuta*		
Snipe	*Gallinago gallinago*		
Jack Snipe	*Lymnocryptes minimus*		
Woodcock	*Scolopax rusticola*		
Curlew	*Numenius arquata*		
Spotted Redshank	*Tringa erythropus*		
Green Sandpiper	*Tringa ochropus*		
Common Sandpiper	*Actitis hypoleucos*		
Great Skua	*Catharacta skua*		
Black-Headed Gull	*Larus ridibundus*		
Sandwich Tern	*Sterna sandviciensis*		
Puffin	*Fratercula arctica*		
Kingfisher	*Alcedo atthis*		
Skylark	*Alaudia arvensis*		
Meadow Pipit	*Anthus pratensis*		
Water Pipit	*Anthus spinoletta*		
Grey Wagtail	*Motacilla cinera*		
White Wagtail	*Motacilla alba*		
Dunnock	*Prunella modularis*		
Alpine Accentor	*Prunella collaris*		
Robin	*Erithacus rubecula*		
Bluethroat	*Luscinia svecica*		
Black Redstart	*Phoenicurus ochruros*		
Ring Ouzel	*Turdus torquatus*		
Fieldfare	*Turdus pilaris*		
Song Thrush	*Turdus philomelos*		
Redwing	*Turdus iliacus*		

Winter Visitiors (cont'd)			
English Name	**Latin/Scientific Name**	**Year Seen**	**Tick**
Mistle Thrush	*Turdus viscivorus*		
Dartford Warbler	*Sylvia undata*		
Chiffchaff	*Phylloscopus collybita*		
Goldcrest	*Regulus regulus*		
Starling	*Sturnus vulgaris*		
Siskin	*Carduelis spinus*		
Hawfinch	*Coccothraustes coccothraustes*		

Vagrants & Accidentals			
English Name	**Latin/Scientific Name**	**Year Seen**	**Tick**
Black-throated Diver	*Gavia arctica*		
Red-necked Grebe	*Podiceps grisegena*		
Slavonian grebe	*Podiceps auritus*		
Swinhoe's Petrel	*Oceanodroma monorhis*		
White Pelican	*Pelacanus onocrotalus*		
Mute Swan	*Cygnus olor*		
Whooper swan	*Cygnus cygnus*		
Bean Goose	*Asnser fabalis*		
White-fronted Goose	*Anser albifrons*		
Ruddy Shelduck	*Tadorna ferruginea*		
Blue-winged Teal	*Anas discors*		
Marbled Teal	*Marmaronetta angustirostris*		
Scaup	*Aythya marila*		
Eider	*Somateria mollissima*		
Long-tailed Duck	*Clangula hyemalis*		
Common Scoter	*Melanitta nigra*		
Goldeneye	*Bucephala clangula*		
Red-breasted Merganser	*Mergus serrator*		
Goosander	*Mergus merganser*		
White-tailed Eagle	*Haliaeetus albicilla*		

Vagrants & Accidentals (cont'd)			
English Name	**Latin/Scientific Name**	**Year Seen**	**Tick**
Short-toed Eagle	*Circaetus gallicus*		
Pallid Harrier	*Circus macrourus*		
Golden Eagle	*Aquila chrysaetos*		
Bonelli's Eagle	*Hieraaetus fasciatus*		
Lesser Kestrel	*Falco naumanni*		
Lanner Falcon	*Falco biarmicus*		
Little Crake	*Porzana parva*		
Baillon's Crake	*Porzana pusilla*		
Corncrake	*Crex crex*		
Little Bustard	*Tetrax tetrax*		
Cream-coloured Courser	*Cursorius cursor*		
Black-winged Pratincole	*Glareola nordmanni*		
Dotterel	*Charadrius morinellus*		
Pectoral Sandpiper	*Calidris melanotos*		
Purple Sandpiper	*Calidris maritima*		
Broad-billed Sandpiper	*Calidris falicinellus*		
Buff-breasted Sandpiper	*Tryngites subruficollis*		
Great Snipe	*Gallinago media*		
Terek Sandpiper	*Xenus cinereus*		
Red-necked Phalarope	*Phalaropus lobatus*		
Arctic Skua	*Stercorarius parasiticus*		
Long-tailed Skua	*Stercorarius longicaudus*		
Common Gull	*Larus canus*		
Herring Gull	*Larus argentatus*		
Great Black-backed Gull	*Larus marinus*		
Kittiwake	*Rissa tridactyla*		
Caspian tern	*Sterna caspia*		
Lesser Crested Tern	*Sterna bengalensis*		
Roseate Tern	*Sterna dougallii*		
Common Tern	*Sterna hirundo*		

Vagrants & Accidentals (cont'd)			
English Name	**Latin/Scientific Name**	**Year Seen**	**Tick**
Guillemot	*Uria aalge*		
Razorbill	*Alca torda*		
Stock Dove	*Columba oenas*		
Great Spotted Cuckoo	*Clamator glandarius*		
Little Owl	*Athene noctua*		
Tawny Owl	*Strix aluco*		
Red-necked Nightjar	*Caprimulgus ruficolis*		
Bar-tailed Desert Lark	*Ammomanes cincturus*		
Calandra Lark	*Melanocorphia calandra*		
Lesser Short-toed Lark	*Calandrella rufescens*		
Woodlark	*Lullula arborea*		
Richard's Pipit	*Anthus novaeseelandiae*		
Olive-backed Pipit	*Anthus hodgsoni*		
Rock Pipit	*Anthus petrosus*		
Citrine Wagtail	*Motacilla citreola*		
Rufous Bush Robin	*Cercotrichas galactotes*		
Savi's Warbler	*Locustella luscinioides*		
Aquatic Warbler	*Acrocephalus paludicola*		
Marsh warbler	*Acrocephalus palustris*		
Orphean Warbler	*Sylvia hortensis*		
Lesser Whitethroat	*Sylvia curruca*		
Yellow-browed Warbler	*Phylloscopus inoratus*		
Red-breasted Flycatcher	*Ficedula parva*		
Collard Flycatcher	*Ficedula albicollis*		
Semi-collard Flycatcher	*Ficedula semitorquata*		
Coal Tit	*Parus ater*		
Wallcreeper	*Tichodroma muraria*		
Short-toed Treecreeper	*Certhia brachydactyla*		
Penduline Tit	*Remiz pendulinus*		
Great Grey Shrike	*Lanius excubitor*		

Vagrants & Accidentals (cont'd)

English Name	Latin/Scientific Name	Year Seen	Tick
Masked Shrike	*Lanius rubicus*		
Jay	*Garrulus glandarius*		
Alpine Chough	*Pyrrhocorax graculus*		
Chough	*Pyrrhocorax pyrrhocorax*		
Jackdaw	*Corvus monedula*		
Rook	*Corvus frugilegus*		
Carrion Crow	*Corvus corone*		
Spotless Starling	*Sturnus unicolor*		
Rose-coloured Starling	*Sturnus roseus*		
Spanish Sparrow	*Passer hispaniolensis*		
Rock Sparrow	*Petronia petronia*		
Snow Finch	*Montifringilla nivalis*		
Redpoll	*Carduelis flammea*		
Trumpeter Finch	*Bucanetes githagineus*		
Scarlet Rosefinch	*Carpodacus erythrinus*		
Bullfinch	*Pyrrhula pyrrhula*		
Snow Bunting	*Plectrophenax nivalis*		
Yellowhammer	*Emberiza citrinella*		
Rock Bunting	*Emberiza cia*		
Little Bunting	*Emberiza pusilla*		

Introduced (I) or Escaped Species (E)

English Name	Latin/Scientific Name	Year Seen	Tick
Pink-Backed Pelican *(E)*	*Pelecanus rufescens*		
Sacred Ibis *(E)*	*Threskiornis aethiopicus*		
African Spoonbill *(E)*	*Plataelea alba*		
Mandarin Duck *(E)*	*Aix galericulata*		
White-headed Duck *(I)*	*Oxyura leucocephala*		
Pheasant *(I)*	*Phasianus colchicus*		
Purple Gallinule *(I)*	*Porphyrio porphyrio*		

THE FLORA AND FAUNA OF MALLORCA

I am only going to touch briefly on this subject as this book is aimed specifically at the bird life of the island. However, there are some interesting wildlife and plants to be found and I would certainly recommend that if time allows to explore the many areas where one can see some spectacular plants especially members of the orchid family. Mallorca has some endemic species of plant such as the Balearic Cyclamen, Balearic Horseshoe Vetch and Balearic St John's Wort which is a relic of the last ice age. The mountain regions have the largest stretches of Holm Oak woods.

There is also a good selection of mammals too. Night drives along the mountain roads have given me Genet, Pine Martin, rodents and nocturnal birds too especially Little Owls which feed on beetles on the roads and Red-legged Partridges scurrying away into cover and on several occasions at Cases Velles a Nightjar on the side of the road.

Mammals are represented by the Vagrant Hedgehog which is a North African species and can be found anywhere on the island and Pine Martins which are usually more difficult to see (although roadkills are fairly common). They can be seen running away into cover as a vehicle approaches especially along the mountain roads. Rabbits and Hares are present and can be found throughout the island. Black Rat, Wood Mouse, House Mouse and the delightful White-toothed Shrew inhabit the island. Common Dormouse is also present but being nocturnal, finding them can be difficult.

Although their status is not fully known both Wild Cat and Genet are present. I have never seen Wild Cat on the island but I was fortunate to have a close view of a Genet on a mountain road just above Cala San Vicente. Weasels can occasionally be seen. There are two kinds of Tortoise on the island - Herman's Tortoise and Spur-thighed Tortoise the latter being confined to restricted areas.

There are four species of non-poisonous snake on the island found mostly in the wooded mountainous areas and the marsh areas. Albufera Marsh is a good site to see snakes in the canals especially from the two bridges adjacent to the footpath which leads down to Bishops 1 and 2 hides. There are Grass Snake, Ladder Snake, False Smooth Snake and the more common Viperine Snake to be found on the island.

Amphibians are well represented and include Lilford's Lizard which is an endemic species Moorish Ghecko, Turkish Ghecko, Marsh Frog, Stripeless Tree Frog, Green Toad and Mallorcan Midwife Toad. A great spot to see the latter two species is from the dam at Cuber Reservoir looking down into the rock pools below. You will certainly hear them. In fact any body of water including hotel pools regularly hold Green Toad.

Butterflies to be found include the beautiful Swallowtail, Clouded Yellow, Cleopatra, Two-tailed Pasha, Camberwell Beauty and the Queen of Spain Frittilery amongst others.

If you have an interest in flowers then the island boasts over twenty seven species of orchid which include Hellibores, Violet Limodore, Sawfly Orchid, Bug Orchid and one of my favourites the Bee Orchid. There is an excellent identification book on flowers entitled *'Wildflowers of the Mediterranean'* by Marjorie Blamey (ISBN 0-7136-7015-0).

BIBLIOGRAPHY

Helbeg 2001 / Jonsson and Felda 2006
Collins Bird Guide - Mullarney / Svenson / Grant / Zetterstrom
Mallorca Culture and Life - Koneman / Verlagsesellschaff
Top 10 Travel - Eye Witness
Mallorca Bird Reports - Hearl / Tillotson / Thompson / Wellings / Hanford
Personal records and sightings - Neville Davies / John L Davies (father)

ACKNOWLEDGEMENTS

I would like to personally thank the following people for their contributions to this book.

Ian Tillotson for the Foreword
Cliff Woodhead for giving me permission to use his photographs
Alan Woodward for giving me permission to use his photograph for the front cover
Mike Cram for the arduous task of checking the bird species
Cindy Kingham for proof reading the book

FURTHER READING

Majorca, Culture and Life	Edda Hammer	ISBN 978-3829025973
Nature Mallorca	Torrens, Ray	ISBN 978-8484781646
Motoring in Spain	Deller, Brian John	ISBN 978 84 611 9278 6

Please send me your sightings (for any species seen during your stay) to: ecologycymru@gmail.com.

Also please take a browse around my web site at: www.ecologycymru.co.uk

USEFUL INFORMATION

Emergency number	112
Medical card web site	www.nhs-services.org.uk
Dialing code for the UK	00 44
24 hour medical service:	Freephone 900 77 76 75 from UK mobiles: 0034 971 70 64 58
British Consul	902 109 356
Fire Brigade	085
Ambulance	061
Police	092
Tourist Office (Puerto Pollensa)	971 865 467
Taxi rank (Puerto Pollensa)	971 866 213
Dawn approximately	06.30 Late April – May
Dusk approximately	20.45
Email:	parc.albufera@gmail.com
Web:	http://mallorcaweb.net/salbufera/